Listening Partner
An Intermediate Course

Osamu Takeuchi
Graeme Todd
Roger Palmer

KINSEIDO

Kinseido Publishing Co., Ltd.
3-21 Kanda Jimbo-cho, Chiyoda-ku,
Tokyo 101-0051, Japan

Copyright © 2009 by Osamu Takeuchi
             Graeme Todd
             Roger Palmer

All rights reserved. No part of this publication may be reproduced, stored in a retrieval system, or transmitted, in any form or by any means, electronic, mechanical, photocopying, recording or otherwise, without the prior permission of the publisher.

First Published 2009 by Kinseido Publishing Co., Ltd.

Cover design Takayuki Minegishi
Text design   Nampoosha Co., Ltd.
Illustrations Natsu Miyazawa
Photography   Graeme Todd

はじめに

　本書は、リスニングを中心とした英語授業で使われることを念頭に、大学1年生〜2年生を対象として編まれた教科書です。大学レベルの英語リスニング用教科書は数多く出版されていますが、本書には類書にない以下のような特徴が含まれています。

1) 大学生にとって興味深いトピックをあつかった会話、ディスカッション、プレゼンテーションなどを聞きながら、具体的なリスニングの方法（リスニング・ストラテジーといいます）について集中的に学ぶことができる。

2) 日本に来た留学生たちを登場人物として設定することで、日本文化についても学びながら、異文化適応の過程を追体験していくことができる。

3) いろいろな種類の英語（たとえば、オーストラリア英語など）に慣れ親しむことができる。

4) リスニング（インプット）に終わらず、自己表現（アウトプット）まで学習をつなげることができる。

　上記1) に関しては、ただ英語を聞き内容を理解するだけではリスニング力は向上しないという考えに基づき、「どのように聞くのか」という視点を学習者のみなさんに持っていただけるよう工夫をしました。2) に関しては、従来の教科書にありがちな日本人が英語圏に留学するというような設定ではなく、日本に来た留学生の目から異文化体験をとらえ、日本文化を参照しながら異文化適応の過程が学べるよう、あえて全Unitにストーリー性を持たせてみました。3) に関しては、昨今TOEIC®に導入されるようになったいろいろな種類の英語に慣れ親しめるよう、登場人物の出身国の設定を多様化する試みを導入してみました。4) に関しては、インプットされた内容をもとにして、自分の考えが表現できるようになるまで、学習者を段階的に誘導していくようタスクを組み立ててみました。

　学習者のみなさんが、上記のような本書の特徴をうまく活用して英語リスニングの方法について理解を深め、継続的にリスニングにチャレンジしていく姿勢を身につけていただけるよう、著者一同、心から願ってやみません。

　最後に、本書の編集にあたり金星堂編集部のみなさんに大変お世話になりました。ここに記して感謝したいと思います。

著者一同

Contents

Unit 1	**Starting Out**	1
	■ 文脈から展開を予測しよう	
Unit 2	**University Life**	7
	■ 語句の言い換えに注意しよう	
Unit 3	**Getting Organized**	13
	■ 問題文や選択肢を先読みしよう	
Unit 4	**Out and About in Kobe**	19
	■ すべてを聞き取る必要はない	
Unit 5	**Misunderstandings**	25
	■ スクリプトで理解を確認しよう	
Unit 6	**Fuji Rock**	31
	■ 仲間と協力しあいながら聞き取り作業をすすめよう	
Unit 7	**Work (part-time jobs)**	37
	■ 要点部分を注意深く聞き取ろう	
Unit 8	**Family Life**	43
	■ 談話標識に気をつけよう	
Unit 9	**The University Festival**	49
	■ 背景知識を利用しよう	
Unit 10	**Society**	55
	■ 音の変化に慣れよう	
Unit 11	**New Year**	61
	■ 固有名詞に着目しよう	
Unit 12	**Clean Living**	67
	■ 視覚情報を利用しよう	
Unit 13	**A Change in the Weather**	73
	■ 語彙を増やそう	
Unit 14	**Packing Up**	79
	■ 数の表現に注意しよう	
Unit 15	**Back Home**	85
	■ 多様な題材をいろいろな人の声で聞いてみよう	

Unit 1

Starting Out
■文脈から展開を予測しよう■

留学（study abroad）先での初めての授業となると不安はピークに達するものです。授業の半分もわからない、先生とどう接して良いのかわからない、自分はこれからどうなるのだろうか？こんな悩みに救いの手を差し伸べてくれるのが友人たちです。友人たちと授業の理解を確かめあったり、学ぶ意義について議論しあったり、そんな楽しいひと時が不安をかき消してくれることでしょう。

Warm Up 1

CD 1-02

よく聞いて、それぞれの写真を一番うまく説明している文をa～dから1つ選びなさい。

1.

a b c d

2.

a b c d

First Listening — First Day of Class

CD1-03

A 会話を聞いて質問に答えなさい。

1. Where do you think Sophie and Erina are?
   - a At the theater
   - b On campus
   - c In a park
   - d In class

2. Why does Sophie start talking to Erina?
   - a Because she is bored
   - b Because she wants to make friends
   - c Because she doesn't understand
   - d Because Erina looks friendly

3. What do Sophie and Erina decide to do?
   - a Talk to each other later
   - b Study Japanese together
   - c Write a report together
   - d Talk about the teacher

Unit 1 Starting Out

B 会話を聞いて質問に答えなさい。　　　　　　　　　　　CD1-04

1. How much of the class did Sophie understand?
   - a About 20%
   - b About 50%
   - c About 90%
   - d All of it

2. Why is Erina's English so good?
   - a She spent a year abroad.
   - b She is from New Zealand.
   - c She studied hard.
   - d She was born in England.

3. When did Sophie arrive in Japan?
   - a Today
   - b A week ago
   - c A few days ago
   - d A month ago

Warm Up 2

よく聞いて、a～cのうちから一番よい応答に１つ○をしなさい。　　CD1-05

1. a   b   c　　　　　　2. a   b   c

3. a   b   c　　　　　　4. a   b   c

Second Listening　Reasons for Studying

CD1-06

A Sophie が言ったことを一番よく描写している文をそれぞれ１つ選びなさい。

1.
   - a She said that she met some other foreign students at lunch.
   - b She said that she talked about the campus all day.
   - c She said that she talked about why she was at university.

2.
   - a She said that she wants to earn as much as she can.
   - b She said that she wants to study as long as she can.
   - c She said that she wants to learn as much as she can.

B Jake が言ったことを一番よく描写している文をそれぞれ1つ選びなさい。

1. a He said that nothing is really important.
   b He said that the future is most important.
   c He said that history is most important.

2. a He said that graduating is going to be a problem.
   b He said that studying electronic engineering is a waste of time.
   c He said that studying history won't help you get a job.

C Shan が言ったことを一番よく描写している文をそれぞれ1つ選びなさい。

1. a He said that he wants to have a good time.
   b He said that he wants to study hard.
   c He said that he wants to join a club.

2. a He said that he met many people today.
   b He said that he has many hobbies.
   c He said that university is not only about studying.

D 次の質問についてグループでディスカッションをしてみましょう（話を始める前に考えをまとめて、それをメモしなさい）。

1. Whose opinion do you agree with most? Sophie's, Jake's or Shan's? Why?
2. What do you put most of your time and effort into at school?

Third Listening — Why I'm Here

CD1-07

A 弱形（弱く発音される部分）に注意して下線をうめなさい。

My name is Jake. I'm an American ¹._____ Pennsylvania. I'm 21 years old, and I've recently started studying electronic engineering ²._____ university in Kyoto, Japan. I'm an exchange student ³._____ will be living here in Japan for a year.

I decided to come here to study because Japan is one of the world leaders in the field ⁴._____ electronic engineering. Japanese technology is especially advanced in ⁵._____ area of robotics. I hope this experience will be useful ⁶._____ my career when I go back to the United States, graduate and start working.

However, I don't plan to be studying all the time. I want to enjoy being in Japan as well. I hope to make friends at the university and have ⁷._____ lively social life. Back ⁸._____ America I played basketball, so I'm thinking ⁹._____ joining the university basketball club. I've heard that joining a club is one of the best ways to make friends here.

Jake

B 大学で学ぶ理由を自分なりに考えて短いパラグラフにまとめなさい。

C Bで書いたパラグラフを使い、自分の考えをクラスに報告しなさい。

Listening Strategy

■文脈から展開を予測しよう■

　文脈から話の展開を予想するというと、何か高度なことをやるように聞こえますが、決して難しいことではありません。我々は、母語での聞き取りでも日常的にこのような行為をおこなっているのです。たとえば、バイトを休みがちの友人の話をしていて、「明日もまた…」といわれると、その後に続くセリフはある程度推測できるはずです。外国語のリスニングでも同じことで、いままでの流れの中で理解できた部分などを参考にして、入ってくるインプットの内容を常に予想・確認しながら処理するのです。

　さて、文脈からの推測のやり方にはいろいろとありますが、ここでは3つほど紹介しておきましょう。

　　　1）スクリプトを利用する
　　　2）キーワードを利用する
　　　3）談話標識を利用する

　まず、ここで言うスクリプトとは、固定化された話の展開パターンのことをさします。たとえば、「くしゃみスクリプト」では、くしゃみをした人に対して、周りの人が Bless you! と言い、これを受けてくしゃみをした人は Thank you. と答えます。このように最初からある程度決まったパターンが存在している場合は、どのようなセリフが Bless you! のあとに出てくるかを推測するのはきわめて容易になります。このようなスクリプトはいくつかありますが（たとえば、お世辞スクリプト、レストラン・スクリプト、断りスクリプトなど）、慣れておいて損はないものです。

　2つ目のキーワードとは、リスニングの際に繰り返し出てくる重要語句をさします。たとえば、Africa, Poverty という単語が繰り返しでていると、おそらくはアフリカの飢餓に関する話題が話されていると予測がつきます。つまり、文脈中に繰り返し出てくる語句は主題と密接に関係すると考えて、これを利用して意味を推測するのです。

　3番目の談話標識（Discourse Marker）とは、話の展開の方向性を教えてくれるサインのようなものです。たとえば、Let me explain my three reasons. <u>Firstly</u>, ... <u>Secondly</u>, ... <u>and finally</u>, ... というと、理由は3つあり、それぞれ、Firstly, Secondly, Finally の後ろに理由が述べられていることが推測できます。下線部のような語句を談話標識と呼びますが、この例のほかにも、付加を示すもの、結論を示すもの、逆接を示すもの、話題の転換を示すものなど、いくつも存在しています。それぞれどのような表現があるのか、一度みなさんで議論してみるのも良いでしょう。

Unit 2

University Life
■語句の言い換えに注意しよう■

どこの国でも新入生が入学する季節の大学キャンパスは活気に溢れるもの。最初の1週間は Freshers' Week（新入生歓迎週間）と呼ばれ、大学のオリエンテーションや施設の利用案内、クラブやサークル活動への勧誘が盛んにおこなわれます。図書館などの施設の利用案内では、Guide から説明を受ける形式が普通です。クラブ、サークルの勧誘では、Freshers' Week Booth が設置され、活動の紹介や参加の受け付けがおこなわれます。

Warm Up 1

CD1-08

よく聞いて、それぞれの写真を一番うまく説明している文を a〜d から1つ選びなさい。

1.

2.

a b c d

a b c d

First Listening   Freshers' Fair

CD1-09

A 会話を聞いて質問に答えなさい。

1. Where are Sophie and Jake?
   - a At a funfair
   - b In class
   - c At the Fresher's Fair
   - d At a music club meeting

2. What kind of music do people in the club mainly play?
   - a Rock and pop
   - b Rock, pop and jazz
   - c Rock and roll
   - d Piano music

3. How does Sophie know where the meeting will be held?
   - a She's been there before.
   - b It's marked on a map.
   - c It's near the campus.
   - d She drew a map.

4. What does the female student do?
   - a She's a player.
   - b She's a coach.
   - c She's a swimmer.
   - d She's a manager.

Unit 2　University Life

B 会話をもう一度聞いて、下線部分を完成させ、その同意表現を選択肢の中から1つ選びなさい。

1. "OK. I'll see if they have a basketball team. _____ you _____."
   a　Have a good time.
   b　See you.
   c　Hope so.

2. "Oh, do you really? _____ good."
   a　Seems interesting.
   b　Great music.
   c　I'll join.

3. "We came third in the league last year. We're not _____."
   a　Poor
   b　All right
   c　Excellent

Warm Up 2

CD1-10

よく聞いて、a〜cのうちから一番よい応答に1つ○をしなさい。

1.　a　b　c　　　　2.　a　b　c

3.　a　b　c　　　　4.　a　b　c

Second Listening　Library Tour

CD1-11

A Jakeが言ったことを一番よく描写している文をそれぞれ1つ選びなさい。

1. a　He said that the library is too busy.
   b　He said that he watches TV when studying.
   c　He said that he's not good at studying in a library.

2. a　He said that TV is very funny.
   b　He said that music helps him concentrate.
   c　He said that he can only concentrate when it is quiet.

B Shan が言ったことを一番よく描写している文をそれぞれ 1 つ選びなさい。

1.
   a   He said that he falls asleep when he tries to study on his bed.
   b   He said that he always studies in bed before going to sleep.
   c   He said that he likes to do other things when he is studying.

2.
   a   He said that he finds it easy to argue with Jake.
   b   He said that he finds it easier to study in the library.
   c   He said that he doesn't like to be alone.

C 会話をもう一度聞いて、下線部分を完成させ、その同意表現を a～c の中から 1 つ選びなさい。

1. "I like listening to music when I study. It helps me _____."
   a   finish it
   b   think clearly
   c   enjoy it

2. "I do both. It depends on _____ I'm in."
   a   what's happening to me
   b   the subject I'm studying
   c   how I feel

3. "Sometimes it's good to be _____ by _____."
   a   in a crowd
   b   in a cafe
   c   with some friends

D 次の質問についてグループでディスカッションをしてみましょう（話を始める前に考えをまとめて、それをメモしなさい）。

1.   Where do you like to study? Why?
2.   What time of day is best for studying?

Unit 2 University Life

Third Listening — My New Circle

CD1-12

A 過去形の語尾（-ed）に注意して下線をうめなさい。

I've ¹._____ a circle. In England we would call it a society or club, but here it's a circle. Anyway, it's a good way to make friends. I only became a member last week, but I've already been to a cherry blossom party and joined a band.

The cherry blossom party was by the Kamogawa river. Some of the circle members went there in the afternoon to reserve a good spot and the rest of us ²._____ in the early evening. We had a barbecue, ³._____ games and sang. It was a fantastic night.

One of the guys ⁴._____ talking about the music he ⁵._____ . His tastes are really similar to mine, like Green Day and Primal Scream. Anyway, he's putting a band together and ⁶._____ if I was interested. I said yes. We'll be getting together to rehearse soon.

Sophie

B 自分が参加しているクラブやサークル活動について短いパラグラフにまとめなさい。

C Bで書いたパラグラフを使い、自分の考えをクラスに報告しなさい。

Listening Strategy

■語句の言い換えに注意しよう■

　英語という言語は、同じ表現や語句を繰り返して利用することを嫌う傾向が強いと言われています。たとえば、President of the US（米国大統領）と言ったかと思うと、次の瞬間、Commander-in-Chief（全軍の最高指揮官：CIC）と言ってみたり、その次には、Head of the Government（行政府の責任者）と表現してみたり、Former Governor/Senator（前知事、前上院議員）と前の役職で呼んでみたり、フルネームや出身地（たとえば a man from Illinois, New Yorker, Texan など）で呼んでみたり、と目まぐるしく呼び方が変わることもよくある現象です。リスニングの際には、このような言い換えに十分注意し、どの表現がどの表現と同意であるのかを把握する必要があります。

　このような言い換え現象は、何も名詞や名詞句表現に限られたものではありません。たとえば、「大きい」を表す形容詞は、英語学習者の場合、big, large 程度しか思いつかないかもしれませんが、母語話者の場合

　　　huge, giant, gigantic, enormous, extensive, massive, vast, tremendous, oversized, overgrown, bulky, great, considerable, immense, colossal, titanic, sizable（順不同）

と色々な単語が口をついて出てきます。また、「あとで会いましょう」というような会話の決まり文句でも、英語学習者は See you later の一本槍でしょうが、母語話者は Get you later, Catch you later, Meet you later といろいろな動詞を使い、表現に幅をもたせる傾向があります。あいさつの表現でも、Hi! や Yo!, Hello! などから始まり、What's up?, How are you?, How are you doing today?, How are you feeling today?, How do you do? と広がりがあります。

　それでは学習者はどのように多様な表現を身につけて、リスニングやスピーキングに利用していけば良いのでしょうか。もっとも良い学習方法は、Thesaurus（シソーラス）、つまり類語辞典を活用することでしょう。シソーラスとは、もともとギリシャ語で「宝庫」を意味する単語が語源となっていますが、まさに表現の宝庫というにふさわしいもので、検索対象になる単語の類似表現（synonymous expression; synonym）がいくつも（辞書によっては例文つきで）紹介されています。ある単語を辞書で引いたら、別の表現はないかなと、ついでにシソーラスも引いてみましょう。そうすることにより、思いがけない表現の宝に出会えるかもしれません。また、類似表現のチェックがおわったら、次は反意表現 (antonym) にも注意してみてください。表現や語句というものは、たくさん知っていても決して邪魔になるようなものではありません。ぜひ、類似語や反意語を利用した「芋づる式」の語彙学習法を利用して、多様な表現を身につけていってください。

Unit **3**

Getting Organized
■問題文や選択肢を先読みしよう■

欧米の大学では、新入生たちは、thrifty shop などと呼ばれるリサイクル店で生活必需品を揃えていくことが多いようです。掲示板に卒業を控えた学生が "Buy my microwave for $300. Call XXX-XXXX." などと宣伝を出している場合も多いので、それを見て電話をすることもあります。日本人の学生は、下宿生活を始めるにあたって新品を揃えることが多いようですが、リサイクル品（second hand）も捨てたものではありません。

Warm Up 1　　　CD1-13

よく聞いて、それぞれの写真を一番うまく説明している文を a〜d から1つ選びなさい。

1.

　a　b　c　d

2.

　　　　　　a　b　c　d

13

First Listening | The Recycle Shop

CD1-14

問題文を先によく読み、その後で会話を聞いて a～d から答えを 1 つ選びなさい。

1. What surprises Shan about the shop?
   - a It's smaller than he expected.
   - b It's bigger than he expected.
   - c It's older than he expected.
   - d It's newer than he expected.

2. What does Shan take to the shop?
   - a Loads of stuff
   - b A list
   - c A chest of drawers
   - d Things he needs

3. What is the first thing Shan asks Sophie about in the shop?
   - a A chest of drawers
   - b A table
   - c A microwave
   - d A vacuum cleaner

4. Why doesn't Sophie like the microwave?
   - a Because of the price
   - b Because of the design
   - c Because of the colour
   - d Because of the quality

5. How much does the vacuum cleaner cost?
　　a　1,000 yen　　　　b　2,000 yen
　　c　3,000 yen　　　　d　4,000 yen

6. What will Sophie ask the shopkeeper about?
　　a　The shop　　　　b　Their kitchen
　　c　A rice cooker　　d　A discount

*W*arm *U*p 2　　　　　　　　　　　　　　CD1-15

よく聞いて、a～cのうちから一番よい応答に1つ○をしなさい。

1.　a　b　c　　　　　2.　a　b　c

3.　a　b　c　　　　　4.　a　b　c

*S*econd *L*istening　What More Do We Need?

CD1-16

A a～cの選択肢を先によく読みなさい。その後で会話を聞いて、Sophieの言ったことを一番よく表す文をそれぞれ1つ選びなさい。

1.　a　She said that they got all of the things they were looking for.
　　b　She said that they bought a table, a microwave and a vacuum cleaner.
　　c　She said that they got a table, a microwave and a washing machine.

2.　a　She said that they don't really need a washing machine.
　　b　She said that they really need a washing machine.
　　c　She said that washing machines were not expensive.

3.　a　She said that the coin laundry is a two-minute ride away.
　　b　She said that the coin laundry is on the other side of town.
　　c　She said that the coin laundry is only two minutes away on foot.

B a〜cの選択肢を先によく読みなさい。その後で会話を聞いて、Jake の言ったことを一番よく表す文をそれぞれ1つ選びなさい。

1. a   He said that they don't really need a washing machine.
   b   He said that he'd rather spend the money on a coin laundry.
   c   He said that it'd be easier if they had a washing machine.

2. a   He said that he doesn't want to wait at the coin laundry.
   b   He said that the coin laundry takes at least two hours.
   c   He said that the coin laundry doesn't take an hour.

3. a   He said that Shan wants to buy a washing machine too.
   b   He said that washing your clothes in a public machine is strange.
   c   He said that coin laundries are interesting.

C 次の質問についてグループでディスカッションをしてみましょう（話を始める前に考えをまとめて、それをメモしなさい）。

1. What have you bought for your room? Where did you buy those things?
2. Do you usually buy new products or old products? Why?

Third Listening: Buying Second-hand Goods

🎧 CD1-17

A 冠詞 (a/an/the) の弱形 に注意して下線をうめなさい。

1. _____ other day Sophie and Jake asked me what I thought about buying second-hand goods. Actually, I'm quite 2. _____ fan of buying used stuff. A lot of 3. _____ furniture I've got in my room is used and so are some of my clothes.

Of course, one benefit of buying second-hand is that it saves you money. I'm 4. _____ student and don't have much spare cash, so that's really important to me. But money's not 5. _____ only reason.

It's also fun and I especially enjoy shopping for used clothes. With new clothes all you can buy are this year's fashions. Used clothes have 6. _____ lot more variety, and that's great if you want to look 7. _____ little different from everybody else.

And I guess the last reason is that recycling anything has got to be good for 8. _____ environment. What's 9. _____ point of throwing 10. _____ perfectly good thing away?

Shan

B 自分が今までに中古で買ったものに関して短いパラグラフにまとめなさい。

C B で書いたパラグラフを使い、自分の考えや経験をクラスに報告しなさい。

Listening Strategy

■問題文や選択肢を先読みしよう■

　受験方略 (Test-taking strategies) の1つに、問題文と選択肢を先読みして、答えとなる情報を焦点化して聞き取る、という方法があります。問題文と選択肢を先に読んでおけば、リスニングの際にすべての情報を聞き取る必要はなく、問題文で尋ねられていることを、しかも選択肢の範囲内で確認するような形式で、身構えしながら特定の情報が流れてくるのを待つことができるのです。

　たとえば Who is going to meet Jack on Sunday? という質問文が示されており、選択肢に a) Mary is b) John is c) Bill is d) Nancy is があるとしましょう。このような場合、他の周辺的な情報（たとえば、場所、時間、服装など）をすべてカットして、ひたすら Jack に、それも日曜日に会うのは誰だ、ということだけに注目して聞いていけばよいわけです。

　我々はリスニングをおこなう際に、たくさんの情報を、しかも同時に処理する必要があります。みなさんも経験があると思いますが、母語でリスニングをしていても、あまりに情報量が多くなってくると、聞き漏らしてしまうという現象が生じます。これは、インプットの量に情報の処理速度が追いつかないために起きる現象です。母語でさえこのような状況が生じるのですから、まだ十分に習得されていない外国語の場合であれば、聞き漏らしが生じても当然なのです。

　日常会話であると、聞き漏らしを想定して、Pardon? とか Say it once again, please. などと相手に繰り返してくれるよう要求したり、Could you speak a bit more slowly, please? などと速度を落すことを要求したり、と対策を講じることが可能です。しかし、リスニングテストの場合はそうはいきません。繰り返すことも速度を落してもらうことも、通常不可能なのです。このような制約があること自体、リスニングテストは不自然な状況で行われている、と言わざるを得ないのですが、ここでテストの批判を始めてみてもしかたがありません。聞き返しや速度調整ができない以上、別の対策を講じる必要があります。その1つが、今回ご紹介した問題・選択肢の先読みなのです。ただし、問題数が多い場合など、問題文と選択肢の両方を先に読むことが時間的に難しい場合もあります。そのような場合、どちらか一方だけでも読んでおけば、まったく情報がなく、焦点化することが不可能な場合よりも有利になります。臨機応変に対応して、すこしでも情報の焦点化が進むよう、工夫をしてみましょう。

Unit 4

Out and About in Kobe
■すべてを聞き取る必要はない■

中国人と中華料理店はどこの国に出かけても必ず見つけることができる、とよく言われます。昔から中国人の海外進出には目覚しいものがあります。また、中華料理店が軒を連ねる中華街（Chinatown）も世界各国に存在していますが、日本では横浜と神戸のそれが特に有名です。後者の神戸は、1995年1月17日に大地震に見舞われましたが、現在は、人的・物的な被害を乗り越えて、不死鳥のように蘇っています。

Warm Up 1　　　CD1-18

よく聞いて、それぞれの写真を一番うまく説明している文をa～dから1つ選びなさい。

1.

a　b　c　d

2.

a　b　c　d

First Listening — Kobe Chinatown

CD1-19

A よく聞いて、会話中に 2 回以上出てくるキーワードを以下の 1 〜 8 のうちから見つけ、チェック（✓）しなさい。

1. _____ Chinese
2. _____ food
3. _____ recognize
4. _____ grandma
5. _____ steamed
6. _____ vegetables
7. _____ delicious
8. _____ starving

B 会話をもう一度聞いて、質問に答えなさい。

1. Where exactly are Jake and Shan at the beginning of the conversation?
   - a In China
   - b Near a Chinese city
   - c By a Chinese gateway
   - d In a Chinese restaurant

2. Which of Shan's relatives came from China?
   - a His sister
   - b His mom
   - c Both his parents
   - d His grandparents

3. What's usually in steamed dumplings?
   - a Pork
   - b Pork and vegetables
   - c Vegetables
   - d Mushrooms and pork

4. Why is Jake so pleased to see Sophie?
   - a Because he can eat
   - b Because he likes her
   - c Because she's late
   - d Because she's sweet

Warm Up 2 CD1-20

よく聞いて、a〜cのうちから一番よい応答に1つ○をしなさい。

1. a b c
2. a b c
3. a b c
4. a b c

Second Listening — Keeping an Earthquake Kit

CD1-21

A よく聞いて、会話中に2回以上出てくるキーワードを以下の1〜8のうちから見つけ、チェック（✓）しなさい。

1. _____ earthquake
2. _____ thousands
3. _____ Kobe
4. _____ leaflet
5. _____ event
6. _____ kit
7. _____ minutes
8. _____ sensible

B Sophie が言ったことを一番よく描写している文をそれぞれ 1 つ選びなさい。

1. a She said that she read about what to do in an earthquake.
   b She said that earthquakes often happen in Kobe.
   c She said that she read about the earthquake in Kobe.

2. a She said that they should keep a supply of fresh fruit.
   b She said that they could go shopping in an emergency.
   c She said that they should keep food, water and medicine.

C Shan が言ったことを一番よく描写している文をそれぞれ 1 つ選びなさい。

1. a He said that it's difficult to walk around Kobe today.
   b He said that the city was rebuilt before the earthquake.
   c He said that he didn't see any earthquake damage in Kobe.

2. a He said that Sophie is calm and sensible.
   b He said that Sophie's opinion seems extreme.
   c He said that he agrees with Sophie.

D 次の質問についてグループでディスカッションをしてみましょう（話を始める前に考えをまとめて、それをメモしなさい）。

1. What kind of natural disasters do you worry about? Why?
2. Have you experienced a big typhoon or other natural disaster? What happened?

Third Listening — Experience of Being in a Natural Disaster

CD1-22

A Have/had/would に注意して下線をうめなさい。

Natural disasters are worrying because they can strike without warning. It's pretty safe where I come from and although I ¹._____ experienced the occasional bad storm, I ²._____ never experienced a powerful hurricane or typhoon. And Pennsylvania is not in an earthquake zone either. But I was in an earthquake once. It happened in California.

I ³._____ slept over at a friend's house, it was early in the morning, and I was still in bed. Suddenly the room began to shake. I ⁴._____ have screamed but I was too scared. As soon as the shaking stopped, I jumped out of bed and ran to find my friend. He didn't seem worried at all. He told me that small earthquakes often happened. Well, if that was a small earthquake, I ⁵._____ hate to be in a big one!

B あなたが今までに経験した自然災害に関して短いパラグラフにまとめなさい。

C Bで書いたパラグラフを使い、自分の経験をクラスに報告しなさい。

Listening Strategy

■すべてを聞き取る必要はない■

　日本人の英語学習者は、リスニングの際に一字一句聞き取ることが大好きなようです。たとえば、リスニングの授業でテープを流して内容理解の問題をやり、その解答や聞き取りのコツ、背景知識などを解説しただけで授業を終えようとすると、必ずと言って良いほど、「先生、スクリプト（ここでは発話を文字起ししたもの）を頂けますか？」という質問を受けることになります。「どうしてスクリプトなんかが必要なの？」と尋ねると、「細かいところが聞き取れていないと不安なんです」、「聞き取れない語があると気持ちが悪くて」というような理由をあげる学生が多いようです。テストでディクテーションを課しているのならいざ知らず、細部を尋ねる出題を一切していない場合でも、同じような要求が後を絶ちません。

　でも、少し考えてみてください。我々は母語のリスニングで、一字一句、ひと言も漏らさずに聞き取りをしているものなのでしょうか？もしそのようなことをしているとしたら、きわめて効率の悪い聞き方をしていることになります。なぜならば、言語には余剰性 (Redundancy) というものがあり、少々聞き漏らしても意味は通じるようにできているからです。また、重要な情報を含む語句が１回だけ現れるということはきわめてまれなことで、たいていの場合、繰り返し、２回、３回 (more than once) と現れてくるので、そこをキーワードとして押さえていけば、細部が少々わからなくても意味はある程度くみ取ることができるようになっています。さらに（リスニングテストでは無理ですが）実際の会話では、聞き漏らしてしまった場合には、「もう一度繰り返してくださいますか？」(Say that once again, please. や Could you repeat it, please? など) と相手に聞き返すことが許されています。２回繰り返してもらってもまだ分からないときには、「別の言い方をしてもらえますか？」(In other words? や Could you paraphrase what you said? など) と、言い換えを求めることも可能です。

　こう考えると、すべての語句に神経を集中させて、全部を聞き取る必要が何もないことがおわかりでしょう。大切なのは、１）何を聞きたいのかという目的意識を持って聞き、２）その目的にあう情報が提示されていると思われる部分に注意を集中して、３）必要な情報だけをとり出す、という戦略的な聞き方 (selective listening) なのです。あとは聞き直す勇気を持てば十分というところでしょうか。

Unit 5

Misunderstandings
■スクリプトで理解を確認しよう■

欧米からの留学生の中には、「わからないことは恥ずかしがらずどんどん質問しなさい」というような自国の社会的なルールに従い、とにかくよく質問する人がいます。「質問をしないことはその話題に興味がないことを示す」と考えている人もいるようです。質問される側も、知らなければ "I don't know." "I have no idea." で済ますようで、日本人のように「答えられずに恥をかいた (embarrassed)」と考える人は少ないようです。

Warm Up 1　　CD1-23

よく聞いて、それぞれの写真を一番うまく説明している文をa～dから1つ選びなさい。

1.

a　b　c　d

2.

a　b　c　d

First Listening — Shimogamo Shrine

CD1-24

A 会話を聞いて質問に答えなさい。

1. What does Erina say about the weather?
   - a   It's beautiful.
   - b   She loves it.
   - c   It isn't hot.
   - d   It's perfect.

2. Which word does Erina translate into English from Japanese?
   - a   Jinja
   - b   Shinto
   - c   Bukkyo
   - d   Shimogamo

3. How does Sophie say she will find out more about shrines and temples?
   - a   She will ask Erina.
   - b   She will write an essay.
   - c   She will get a book.
   - d   She will ask her teacher.

4. What does Erina wish she could do?
   - a   Study more about British culture.
   - b   Give Sophie better answers.
   - c   Ask Sophie more questions.
   - d   Take a walk in the woods.

B 下線部をうめたあと、その答えが正しいかスクリプトを使って確認しなさい。

1. How does Sophie ask for the name of the historical area they are visiting?
   She says, "So what's _____ _____ _____ _____?"

2. When Erina says, "It is a kind of World Heritage Site", how does Sophie respond?
   She says, "Really? _____ _____."

3. How does Erina respond to the question, "So who built this place originally?"
   She says, "Perhaps we should go to that shop and _____ _____ _____ _____."

4. How does Sophie thank Erina for taking her to the shrine?
   She says, "I'm so _____ _____ _____ _____ _____."

Warm Up 2

CD1-25

よく聞いて、a～cのうちから一番よい応答に1つ○をしなさい。

1. a   b   c   2. a   b   c

3. a   b   c   4. a   b   c

Second Listening Questions

CD1-26

A Sophie が言ったことを一番よく描写している文をそれぞれ1つ選びなさい。

1. a She said that Erina was telling funny jokes at the shrine.
   b She said that Erina began to behave a little strangely.
   c She said that Erina's acting was very interesting.

2. a She said that her questions were to show that she was interested.
   b She said that Erina wanted to talk about the shrine.
   c She said that Erina knew all the answers to her questions.

B Shan が言ったことを一番よく描写している文をそれぞれ１つ選びなさい。

1. a He asked Sophie if she was upset.
    b He asked about how Erina had answered Sophie's questions.
    c He asked about what had upset Erina.

2. a He said that Sophie should say sorry to Erina.
    b He said that Sophie should not apologize to Erina.
    c He said that Sophie should try to embarrass Erina more.

C 下線部をうめたあと、その答えが正しいかスクリプトを使って確認しなさい。

1. How does Shan ask about Erina's behaviour?
    He says, "What _____ _____ _____ funny?"

2. When Sophie asks, "What do you think?", how does Shan respond?
    He says, "Yeah, one of my friends was talking about this _____ _____ _____."

3. How does Sophie respond when Shan says, "It can be embarrassing for Japanese when they don't know the answers."
    She says, "What's _____ _____ _____, I don't know?"

4. What does Shan say about how Erina felt?
    He says, "She probably felt that she wasn't _____ _____ _____ properly."

D 次の質問についてグループでディスカッションをしましょう（話を始める前に考えをまとめて、それをメモしなさい）。

1. What kinds of situations make you feel embarrassed? Why?
2. Tell a story about an embarrassing situation that happened to you or a friend.

Third Listening — Differences

A 後ろに母音が続く場合の /t/ と /d/ は、後ろに子音が続く場合の /t/ と /d/ と発音が異なります。この点に注意しながら下線をうめなさい。

When I first 1._____ in Japan I was fascinated by all the differences I could see. The 2._____ was different, the houses were different, and so were the shops. I'd never tried food like *okonomiyaki*, I loved new experiences like sitting on tatami, and really 3._____ visiting Japanese department stores. But the longer I stay here the more I become interested in the way people think, communicate and behave. At 4._____ I assumed that 5._____ for the language there wasn't much difference between myself and 6._____ of the Japanese people I met. 7._____ now I'm not so sure. Now I think social rules are much more important. To make the most of my time in Japan I think I 8._____ to learn more about this aspect of the culture.

B あなたはどのような社会的なルールに従いますか。2, 3 例をあげながら短いパラグラフにまとめなさい。

C B で書いたパラグラフを使い、自分の考えをクラスに報告しなさい。

Listening Strategy

■スクリプトで理解を確認しよう■

　Unit 4 で「すべてを完全に聞き取る必要はない」ということをお話しました。たしかに実際のコミュニケーションの場面ではそうなのですが、英語学習という側面に視点を移すと、ちょっと違ったお話をする必要があります。その理由は、英語学習のためには、「何回か聞いた後に理解できないところはスクリプトで必ず確認した方がよい」からなのです。

　英語圏に留学することなく、日本国内で学びながら高い英語運用力を身につけた「達人」たちの研究*によると、彼らの多くは何回も繰り返して同じ英語の番組や映画を聞き、どうしても理解できないところが残れば、スクリプトで確認したり、ネイティブスピーカーにそこだけ教えてもらったりして、不明箇所をなくしていく努力をしていたようです。そうすることにより、細かな音の変化や音の脱落に慣れていったり、固有名詞やイディオムを学習したりと、英語知識のデータベースを拡げていくことが可能になるからです。

　ただ、はじめからスクリプトを見ながら英語を聞くのは絶対に禁物のようです。人間は目から入ってくる文字の情報に強く影響を受ける傾向があり、文字と音声を同時に提示されると、どうしても文字の方に引きずられてしまいがちになります。そうすると、実際には目から入ってきた文字情報を読んでいるだけなのに、あたかも音声を聞いて内容を理解しているような錯覚にとらわれてしまいます。このような文字と音声の併用練習を続けていると、リスニング力を伸ばすつもりなのにリーディング力が伸びた、というような笑うに笑えない結果をもたらす場合もありうるのです。

　皆さんも経験があると思いますが、DVD 版の映画などで、字幕を見ながら英語の音声を聞いていると、まるでその映画のすべてが理解できているかのような錯覚にとらわれることがあります。でも、これは上記の説明からわかるように、文字（字幕）の力のおかげなのです。だからこそ、リスニング力を本当に伸ばしたいと思う方には、まずは数回、神経を集中させて音声のみを聞き、どうしてもわからない箇所があれば、あとからスクリプトや字幕でその箇所を確認するというような地道な学習法を強くお薦めしたいと思います。

*たとえば、『達人の英語学習法—データが語る効果的な外国語学習法とは』（竹内 理著、草思社）などが参考になります。

Unit 6

Fuji Rock

■仲間と協力しあいながら聞き取り作業をすすめよう■

夏になると、キャンプや海水浴と屋外での活動に参加する機会が増えていきます。野外コンサートもその1つでしょう。海外では、英国で行われるグラストンベリー・フェスティバルが知られていますが、日本ではフジ・ロックフェスティバルが有名です。ところで、音楽というものは、その人が生まれ育った世代を象徴するものとも言われています。皆さんはどんな音楽を聞きますか？ご両親や兄弟はどんな音楽を聞いているのでしょうか？これを機会に話し合ってみると良いでしょう。

Warm Up 1

CD1-28

よく聞いて、それぞれの写真を一番うまく説明している文をa～dから1つ選びなさい。

1.

a　b　c　d

2.

a　b　c　d

First Listening — Arriving

🎧 CD1-29

A 会話をよく聞き、質問に答えなさい。

1. Where are Sophie and Ryuhei?
   - a At the ticket gate
   - b At the campsite
   - c On the bus
   - d On the stage

2. What do Sophie and Ryuhei decide to do?
   - a Buy their tickets
   - b Relax
   - c Wait for their friends
   - d Put up their tent

3. According to Ryuhei, what information is true about Fuji Rock?
   - a It's a bigger festival than Glastonbury in England.
   - b It's the most famous music festival in Japan.
   - c It started more than ten years ago.
   - d It always rains.

4. What does Sophie say she wants to do?
   - a Check out of the campsite
   - b Listen to some Japanese bands
   - c Buy some CDs
   - d Listen to some punk rock

B ペアを作り協力して質問に答えなさい。1から5については、会話をよく聞き左の文字列を並びかえてバンド名になるようにしなさい。6から9に関しては、会話をよく聞き下線を適語でうめなさい。

The Names of the Bands:

1. The star hueelb = The _____ _____
2. The sermoan = The _____
3. slarmp crimea = _____ _____
4. vistra = _____
5. The non-scamgor = The _____

6. Ryuhei and Sophie both want to see _____ .
7. Sophie has two CDs by _____ .
8. Two guys in _____ used to be in _____ .
9. _____ sounded a bit like _____ .

Warm Up 2
CD1-30

よく聞いて、a～cのうちから一番よい応答に1つ○をしなさい。

1. a b c   2. a b c

3. a b c   4. a b c

Second Listening What Did You Think?

CD1-31

A Sophie が言ったことを一番よく描写している文をそれぞれ1つ選びなさい。

1. a She said that punk is out-of-date.
   b She said that her dad liked punk.
   c She said that punk is too basic.

2. a She said that her dad used to call her Abba.
   b She said that Little Dancing Queen was her nickname.
   c She said that she used to enjoy dancing to Abba's music.

B Ryuhei が言ったことを一番よく描写している文をそれぞれ 1 つ選びなさい。

1. a He said that he has always been a big fan of punk music.
   b He said that he grew up listening to his father's music.
   c He said that he likes punk because his brother used to listen to it.

2. a He said that Sophie's nickname wasn't so bad.
   b He said that Sophie's childhood nickname was strange.
   c He said that he's going to call Sophie, Waterloo.

C ペアを作り一緒に会話を聞いて、下線部を協力してうめなさい。

Ryuhei: My dad (1) _____ didn't listen to punk! Anyway, I love the (2) _____ , the (3) _____ , ... it's just great. You get (4) _____ of listening to silly love songs.

Sophie: So love songs are (5) _____ , are they?

Ryuhei: I didn't mean that... .

Sophie: I know, ... I was only (6) _____ .

Ryuhei: Oh, right. So what kind of music did you (7) _____ listening to?

Sophie: My dad's.

Ryuhei: You mean punk?

Sophie: No, he was the (8) _____ age but he didn't listen to it much. Actually, he was a (9) _____ Abba fan. Have you (10) _____ of them?

D 次の質問についてグループでディスカッションをしてみよう（話を始める前に考えをまとめて、それをメモしなさい）。

1. Which bands have you seen live? Where and when did you see them?
2. What kind of music do you listen to these days? What do you like about it?

Third Listening — No Music, No Fun!

A 音の変化（弱形）に注意して下線部をうめなさい。

Music is an important part of ^{1.}_____ life and I don't know what I'd do without it. "No music, no life." say some people. Well, ^{2.}_____ wouldn't go that far but do think, "No music, no fun!"

I think the greatest invention ^{3.}_____ the 20th century was the portable tape player. Of course, no one uses them now ^{4.}_____ I take a modern version, an MP3 player, with me everywhere I go. It's fantastic. I ^{5.}_____ carry enough music in my pocket to last me for three days without having to listen to the same song twice. And if I ever want to listen to something else ^{6.}_____ a change I can play radio programs downloaded from the internet.

When I'm at home I ^{7.}_____ plug my player into my speaker system and the music continues. It was expensive but I haven't regretted buying ^{8.}_____ for a moment. In fact, I think it's the best thing I ever bought.

B 次のいずれかの話題を選び、短いパラグラフにまとめなさい。

1. あなたの人生における音楽の重要性について
2. いままでで一番良い買い物

C Bで書いたパラグラフを使い、自分の考えや経験をクラスに報告しなさい。

Listening Strategy

■仲間と協力しあいながら聞き取り作業をすすめよう■

　英語学習というと、1人でコツコツ積み上げていく孤独な作業のようなイメージがつきまといます。確かに、個人で地道な努力を重ねていくという側面もあるのですが、最近では、仲間と協力しあいながら学習をすすめる「協働学習」という考え方を英語学習にも持ち込む傾向があります。「もう少しで分かりそうだけど分からない」というような部分を仲間からの手助けやヒント（これを「足場」といいます）を借りて克服していく。思い違いをしている仲間を、ちょっとした足場を提供してあげることで助けてあげる。あるいは、英語学習のやり方を、自分より英語がよく出来る仲間から教えてもらう。こういう「協働作業」が学習を飛躍的に向上させる、という考え方が広く支持されるようになっているのです。

　ただ、「協働学習」はそんなに簡単に出来るものではありません。お互いにいくつかのルールを守りながら作業を行う必要があります。まず注意しなければいけないのは、「答えを見せあい、はやく終わってしまおう」という考え方を捨てることです。大切なのは答えという結果ではなく、その答えにどうやって到達したのかという方法を共有すること。産物ではなく過程に着目しなければいけないのです。これと関連して、「よく出来る1人に作業を押しつけない」ことも大切になります。1人が作業の全過程を独占してしまい、すべての答えを導き出しているようでは、これは「協働」ではなくってしまいます。また、「足場」の提供の方法も重要になります。たとえば、穴埋めのディクテーションをしている際に、「そこは～ing の形だよ」とストレートに言うかわりに、「そこは前置詞の後だから動詞の原形は続かないのでは」と投げかけて、相手に考えさせるような工夫が必要なのです。

　ところで「協働学習」というのは、出来る学生が「プチ教師」になり、他の学生を教え、導くようなシステムなのでしょうか。知識や方法は、あくまでも「高い」ところから「低い」ところへ流れていくのでしょうか。実はそうではなく、英語力の高い学生の方も、他の学生の投げかけた質問を通して思いがけない発見をしたり、知識が整理できたりすることもよくあるのです。理解や気づきが相互に生じること、これが「協働学習」の大原則になります。

Unit 7

Work (part-time jobs)
■要点部分を注意深く聞き取ろう■

大学生にもなるとアルバイト（ドイツ語起源の和製英語です）に精を出す人も多いようです。でも、どうぜ卒業後は嫌でも働かなければなりません。そう考えると、勉強や他の体験ができる最後のチャンスかもしれない大学生になったのに、なぜアルバイトに精を出さねばいけないのか疑問に思って当然でしょう。本文中の留学生たちも、この疑問への答えを真剣に考えているようです。

Warm Up 1　　　　　CD1-33

よく聞いて、それぞれの写真を一番うまく説明している文を a～d から1つ選びなさい。

1.

a　b　c　d

2.

a　b　c　d

First Listening — Jake's Part-time Job

CD1-34

A 会話をよく聞き、要点をよく把握して、質問に答えなさい。

1. What is the main topic of the conversation?
   a   The kinds of drinks they like.
   b   Part-time jobs that Kamei-san does now.
   c   Part-time jobs that Kamei-san used to do.
   d   Part-time jobs that Jake used to do.

2. What does Kamei-san say about her part-time jobs?
   a   She enjoyed doing both her part-time jobs.
   b   She didn't enjoy shouting in the movie theater.
   c   She liked working at the gas station in summer.
   d   She enjoyed working in a movie theater.

B もう一度会話を聞いて、質問に答えなさい。

1. Why does Jake choose the topic of part-time jobs?
   a   Because he has finished talking about drinks.
   b   Because he does not want a weak topic.
   c   Because it is in the textbook.
   d   Because he thinks Kamei-san will be interested in it.

Unit 7 Work (part-time jobs)

2. What is the first question Jake asks about part-time jobs?
   a   Would you like a drink?
   b   Do you have a part-time job?
   c   Have you ever had a part-time job?
   d   What did you do?

3. Why didn't she enjoy working at the gas station?
   a   Because she didn't like working outside.
   b   Because the pay was too low.
   c   Because her voice was too quiet.
   d   Because she caught colds in winter.

4. What did Kamei-san enjoy about working at the movie theater?
   a   She enjoyed it for six months.
   b   She enjoyed watching movies for free.
   c   She enjoyed selling tickets.
   d   She enjoyed getting cheaper tickets.

Warm Up 2

CD1-35

よく聞いて、a～cのうちから一番よい応答に1つ○をしなさい。

1. a   b   c   2. a   b   c

3. a   b   c   4. a   b   c

Second Listening　To Work or Not to Work?

CD1-36

A 会話をよく聞き、要点をよく把握して、質問に答えなさい。

1. What are Jake's reasons for working part-time?
   a   It's always a lot of fun and he needs the money.
   b   It's good experience and the extra money is useful.
   c   He's got a lot of free time and he enjoys the traveling.

2. What reasons does Sophie give for not wanting a part-time job?
  a Because she has more than enough money and wants to study.
  b Because she is not allowed to work in Japan.
  c Because she doesn't have the time or energy to study and work.

B Jake が言ったことを一番よく描写している文をそれぞれ1つ選びなさい。

1. a He said that not all of his students are as interesting as Kamei-san.
  b He said that doing his part-time job is always a lot of fun.
  c He said that he wishes he didn't have to work so many hours.

2. a He said that you need to spend more time on study than work.
  b He said that if you work too hard you lose your balance.
  c He said that you need to get the balance between work and study right.

C Sophie が言ったことを一番よく描写している文をそれぞれ1つ選びなさい。

1. a She said that she is looking for a job.
  b She said that she is in Japan to study.
  c She said that she has already retired.

2. a She said that Shan is lucky because he does not need to work.
  b She said that Shan is lucky because he is a simple person.
  c She said that Shan is lucky because he does not need to study.

D 次の質問についてグループでディスカッションをしてみましょう（話を始める前に考えをまとめて、それをメモしなさい）。

1. What kind of job would you advise a student to do?

2. What's the right balance between work and study? How many hours a week do you think students should work?

Unit 7 Work (part-time jobs)

Third Listening — Working at University

CD1-37

A 名詞が２つ続いた場合、アクセントの置き方が変わる場合があります。この点に注意しながら下線部をうめなさい。

In America most students take ¹._____ - _____ jobs when they are at college. I always had a job when I was studying in the United States so it was natural for me to look for a job here as well. In the last two years I've worked as a ²._____ _____ , as a waiter, and as a ³._____ _____ . I think that was my worst job. I really hated it. I had to go out in all sorts of weather, never got to bed before 1 o'clock in the morning, and was always tired. The best job I had was in a ⁴._____ _____ . It wasn't often busy and so I didn't have much to do. I spent most of my time there doing ⁵._____ . I used to study and get paid at the same time. That was great. And the pay was really good too!

B いままで経験した仕事（アルバイトなど）の良かった点と悪かった点に関して短いパラグラフにまとめなさい。

C Bで書いたパラグラフを使い、自分の考えをクラスに報告しなさい。

Listening Strategy

■要点部分を注意深く聞き取ろう■

　「要点部分を注意深く聞き取ろう」と一口でいいますが、なかなかこれは難しい作業であることは間違いないでしょう。「要点がどこなのか分からないから困っているんだ」とか「どこが要点か始めから分かっていたら誰も苦労しないよ」という声が聞こえてきそうです。このような文句が出るのもしごく当然のことなので、ここでは少しでも要点がつかみやすくなるよう、「要点の見つけ方」について、いくつかアドバイスをしてみましょう。

　まず、トピックセンテンスの概念を応用してみてはどうでしょうか。トピックセンテンスとは、英作文などでよく指摘される概念ですが、それぞれのパラグラフの先頭（まれに最後）に位置し、そのパラグラフ全体のまとめの役割をしている文のことをさします。この文が理解できれば、詳細は聞き漏らしても、そのパラグラフが何について述べられているのか、比較的容易に推測することができます。この原則を利用すると、リスニングの際にも、少し長めのポーズでパラグラフが切り替えられた時、次に続く最初の文に注意するというストラテジーを利用することが可能なのです。

　次に、What I would like to emphasize here is ...（私がここで強調したいのは...です）のような構文に気をつけましょう。このような構文は専門的には「疑似分裂文」と言いますが、聞き手にとって重要なポイントが理解しやすいように、話し手が提供するフレームのようなものです。疑似分裂文以外にも、It is ... that ~（~なのは...です）などの「強調構文」が同じようなフレームの役割を果たす時があります。

　3つ目としては、繰り返し出てくる語句に注意すると良いでしょう。口語では、よほどの理由（たとえば時間制限）がない限り、相手が聞き漏らしても大丈夫なように、重要なポイントを繰り返し説明する傾向があります。そこで、何度も出てくる単語や表現は、要点と関連する傾向が高いと言われています。

　この他にも、Unit 8のコラムでも詳述しますが、談話標識の利用なども、要点の聞き取りには有効です。「要点がどこかなんてわからない」と始めからあきらめたりせずに、上述のような方法を一度試みてみてはいかがでしょうか？

Unit 8

Family Life
■談話標識に気をつけよう■

父親の単身赴任のために家族が離れて暮らす、ということは日本では比較的よくある現象の1つです。しかし海外から来た留学生の目には、これが奇異に映ることもよくあります。このように、ものの見方がわかれた場合に大切なのは、自分の考え方を相手に押しつけないという大原則。So many men, so many minds. ということわざがあるように、考え方は違うもの。お互いの違いを認めて、はじめてコミュニケーションはスタートすると覚えておきましょう。

Warm Up 1　　　　　　　　　　　　　　　　　　　CD1-38

よく聞いて、それぞれの写真を一番うまく説明している文をa〜dから1つ選びなさい。

1.

2.

a　b　c　d　　　　　　a　b　c　d

First Listening — Visiting a Friend's Family

CD1-39

A 談話標識（p.48 コラム参照）に注意しながら会話をよく聞きなさい。

1. How does Sophie introduce the topic of Akiko's family life?
   - a Actually
   - b By the way
   - c I mean
   - d Well

2. How does Akiko start to explain about her father's situation?
   - a Actually
   - b You see
   - c You know
   - d Well

B 会話をもう一度聞いて、質問に答えなさい。

1. When Sophie says the "cooking is amazing," what does she mean?
   - a She is surprised that the food was good.
   - b She expected the food to be good.
   - c She didn't really enjoy the food.
   - d She is impressed because the food was good.

2. How often does Akiko's father come home?
   - a Only two times a year
   - b Every two years
   - c Two or three times a year
   - d Once a year in summer

3. Why did Akiko stop moving to different places with her father?
   a   Because of her father's job
   b   Because of her education
   c   Because of the situation in Shanghai
   d   Because of her mother's cooking

4. When will Sophie visit again?
   a   When she's invited.
   b   When she feels like it.
   c   When there's a bus.
   d   When Akiko's mother asks her.

Warm Up 2

CD1-40

よく聞いて、a～cのうちから一番よい応答に1つ○をしなさい。

1. a   b   c   2. a   b   c

3. a   b   c   4. a   b   c

Second Listening Family Life

CD1-41

A 下線部を談話標識でうめなさい。

Sophie: Jake, did you move around much when you were a child? _____ , like live in different places?

Jake: Yeah. _____ , I changed school several times because of my dad's job. And then my parents got divorced, _____ , so we moved again.

Sophie: Was it difficult, moving so many times?

Jake: _____ , at first it was, but I became pretty good at making new friends. _____ , I had to.

B Sophie が言ったことを一番よく描写している文をそれぞれ1つ選びなさい。

1. a She said that she only attended two different schools.
   b She said that she only moved house twice.
   c She said that she went to the same school till she was eighteen.

2. a She said that it's normal for grown-ups to look after their parents.
   b She said that it's natural for adults to worry about their children.
   c She said that it's natural for adults to live away from their parents.

C Jake が言ったことを一番よく描写している文をそれぞれ1つ選びなさい。

1. a He said that he never got used to moving around.
   b He said that he was used to moving around.
   c He said that he really enjoyed moving around a lot.

2. a He said that he didn't see his father after his parents split up.
   b He said that he lived with his mother after his parents divorced.
   c He said that he lived on his own after his parents divorced.

D 次の質問についてグループでディスカッションをしてみましょう（話を始める前に考えをまとめて、それをメモしなさい）。

1. Have you ever moved house? Tell a partner about it.
2. If you move house in the future, where would you like to live?

Third Listening — The Importance of Family

CD1-42

A "th" の2種類の音に注意して下線を適語でうめなさい。

I've been away from home for about six months now and at first I didn't ¹_____ I'd miss my family. In England I didn't spend much time with my parents, but now, sometimes I would really like to talk to ²_____ about what I'm doing.

It's made me feel ³_____ to be part of a family. When I was small, Mum and Dad did everything for me. Speaking to Akiko and Jake made me appreciate how lucky I am ⁴_____ my parents were always ⁵_____ when I was growing up.

And there's another ⁶_____ about family. It's not just that I miss them and depend on them. I think it's something more than that — perhaps ⁷_____ sense of security. Your family knows everything about you, which means you can be yourself when you are with them. Maybe ⁸_____ are the only people who really know you.

B 家族がなぜ重要なのか、短いパラグラフにまとめなさい。

C Bで書いたパラグラフを使い、自分の体験をクラスに報告しなさい。

Listening Strategy

■談話標識に気をつけよう■

　Unit 1 のコラムでも説明したように、談話標識 (Discourse Marker) とは、話の展開の方向性を教えてくれるサインのようなものです。次に来る情報はどのようなものだろうか、例があといくつ提示されるのだろうか、話題はいつ変わるのだろうか。こう言った情報を聞き手にあらかじめ教えてくれるのが、この談話標識なのです。以下にその例をいくつか示してみましょう。

　まず、「例示」の談話標識には Unit 1 のコラムで説明した Firstly..., Secondly..., Finally... などのほかに、「今から例を示しますよ」ということを伝えるために、

　　　　for example, for instance, such as

などがあります。ちなみに書き言葉では、ラテン語の省略形 e.g. (exempli gratia = for the sake of example) を使って談話標識とすることもあります。

　情報の「追加」を聞き手に教えるための談話標識としては、

　　　　in addition, moreover, furthermore, then

などが考えられます。He is an alumnus, too.（彼もまた同窓生なんですよ）の too のように文の末尾に添えて、あとから「追加」を示す場合もよく見られます。また、「結論」が次に続くことを聞き手に示すためには、

　　　　as a result, in conclusion, consequently, accordingly, thus, therefore,

などがよく使われています。口語では、so なども「結論」の談話標識として通用します。

　いままでの説明と逆の情報が次に来ることを示すためには、

　　　　on the other hand, on the contrary, however, but

などが使われます。このような語句に気がついたら、今までとは180度（少し大げさですが）違う話が次に出てくるかもしれない、と身構えておきましょう。最後に（この言葉自体も実は談話標識なのですが）、話題の「転換」を図るには、now, by the way などがよく使われます。突然今までと違うことを言ったり、新しい話題を導入したりする場合には、You know what?（そうそう知ってる？）とうような言い方も口語表現としてあります。

　上記のような談話標識をしっかりと覚えておくと、リスニングの際に、次にくる内容を予測したり、重要な情報のありかを探ったりすることが比較的簡単にできるようになります。みなさんも、一度、談話標識に着目したリスニングをしてみてはどうでしょうか？

Unit 9

The University Festival
■背景知識を利用しよう■

学園祭（university festival）になると、キャンパスのあちらこちらに店が立ちならび、色々な食べ物が売られます。その際、純和風のお好み焼きやたこ焼きとならんで人気なのがフライド・ポテト（French fries）やハンバーガー (hamburger) などのアメリカン・ファーストフード。一方で、アメリカやイギリスの大学の食堂では寿司 (sushi) が売られて大人気とか。人間は自分の国の味と異なるものを求めるものなのでしょうか。

Warm Up 1　　　CD2-01

よく聞いて、それぞれの写真を一番うまく説明している文を a～d から1つ選びなさい。

1.

2.

a　b　c　d　　　　a　b　c　d

First Listening — On the Stall

▶▶▶ リスニング前活動

Jake は学園祭の模擬店で食べ物を売っています。会話を聞く前に、この状況に関する背景知識を確認してみましょう。

1. What country is Jake from?
   a England
   b Australia
   c USA

2. Which of these foods are American? Check more than one.
   _____ Hot dogs   _____ Croissants
   _____ Fish and chips   _____ Hamburgers
   _____ Spaghetti   _____ Spring rolls

3. Who usually operates the stalls at a university festival?
   a Professors
   b Clubs and circles
   c Private companies

◀◀◀ リスニング後活動   CD2-02

■ 会話をよく聞き、質問に答えなさい。

1. What is something the other stalls will NOT be selling?
   a Fried noodles   b Fried chicken
   c Hamburgers   d Takoyaki

2. What will the club do with the money?
   a Spend it on equipment and a party
   b Save part of it and spend the rest on equipment
   c Buy food and drink and save the rest
   d Spend it on equipment for a party

3. How does Jake like to eat hamburgers?
    a   With a Coke and fries
    b   With onions, ketchup, salad, mayonnaise, mustard and pickles
    c   With fried onions, ketchup and mustard
    d   With onions, mayonnaise and mustard

4. What words does Jake use when he asks for the money?
    a   That's 330 yen, please.
    b   It's 300 yen a piece, sir.
    c   It's 330 yen if you please, sir.
    d   That's 300 yen, please, sir.

Warm Up 2   CD2-03

よく聞いて、a〜cのうちから一番よい応答に1つ○をしなさい。

1. a   b   c   2. a   b   c

3. a   b   c   4. a   b   c

Second Listening   Who Doesn't Like Hamburgers?

▶▶▶ リスニング前活動

SophieとShanはコーヒーショップでアメリカンフードの人気について話をしています。会話を聞く前に、この状況についての背景知識について確認してみましょう。

1. Who was selling food at the festival?
    a   Sophie
    b   Jake
    c   Shan

2. Which of these are styles of coffee? Check more than one.

   _____ Chai   _____ Earl Grey
   _____ Cappuccino   _____ Iced
   _____ Latte   _____ Espresso

3. Which food is generally considered to be unhealthy?
   a Hamburgers
   b Sashimi
   c Salad

◀◀◀ リスニング後活動   CD2-04

A Sophie が言ったことを一番よく描写している文をそれぞれ1つ選びなさい。

1. a She said that she will buy the coffee.
   b She said that she will find a table.
   c She said that Shan should get the coffee.

2. a She said that Jake's hamburgers were expensive and tasteless.
   b She said that a man with a hamburger tried to hurt her.
   c She said that hamburgers are unhealthy and not delicious.

B Shan が言ったことを一番よく描写している文をそれぞれ1つ選びなさい。

1. a He said that eating hamburgers will not hurt you.
   b He said that people don't usually eat hamburgers at festivals.
   c He said that eating the occasional hamburger isn't unhealthy.

2. a He said that people shouldn't be allowed to eat cake.
   b He said that people are free to eat any food they like.
   c He said that delicious food is often unhealthy.

C 次の質問についてグループでディスカッションをしてみましょう（話を始める前に考えをまとめて、それをメモしなさい）。

1. How often do you eat American-style fast food?
2. What foods do you avoid because you think they are either unhealthy or not delicious?

Unit 9 The University Festival

Third Listening — A Positive Experience

CD2-05

A 短縮形に注意しながら会話を聞き下線部をうめなさい（真ん中の２つは例として最初からうめてあります）。

It was really fun selling hamburgers at the university festival. I was glad that they were popular. It was my idea to do it, and it would have (1. _____) been embarrassing if we had not (2. _____) made any money. I really did not want to let down my friends from the circle.

Being in the circle has (3. _____) been a really positive experience for me for a number of reasons. It has (It's) helped me to improve my Japanese. I speak more Japanese with my circle friends than at any other time. And my friends have (4. _____) given me a lot of support, too. When I have (I've) had a problem, they have (5. _____) always helped me deal with it. And, of course, being involved in the training and games has been great.

University is (6. _____) more than just formal education. I think I have (7. _____) learned as much from my circle friends as I have from my classes. And not surprisingly, it has (8. _____) been a lot more fun as well!

B あなたが参加しているクラブやサークルについて、それがどのように自分にとって良い経験となっているのか、短いパラグラフにまとめなさい。

C Bで書いたパラグラフを使い、自分の考えをクラスに報告しなさい。

Listening Strategy

■背景知識を利用しよう■

　リスニングの際に重要な役割を果たすのが背景知識です。トピックに関する背景知識が欠けていると、何の話がこれから展開されるのか予想することがとても難しくなります。たとえば、Today, I am going to talk about "Gini coefficient". と英語の講義の冒頭で言われたとしましょう。おそらく、その瞬間、大多数の学習者が「？」を頭に浮かべてしまうことになるでしょう。なぜなら、"Gini coefficient" について背景知識がまったくないからです。心理学や統計学を学んでいる学生さんの中には coefficient だから何かの「係数」だなと推測できる人もいるでしょう。でも Gini の部分がわかりません。ここに経済学の知識が豊富な学生がいたとしましょう。彼（彼女）は「なるほど。今日はジニー係数の話か。すると所得格差だな。」と、すでに講義の概要を予測することが可能となります。あとは、耳から入ってくる英語を聞きながら、自分の予測を確認していく作業をすれば良いだけです。話の途中で今まで聞いたことのない国の例を出されても、トピックの概要が分かっているので、それほど慌てる必要はありません。

　北米の大学へ留学する際に受ける TOEFL® などのテストでは、講義調の聞き取り問題が出題される場合も多いのですが、その際にも背景知識が大いに手助けになります。こういう理由から、「留学のためにリスニング力をもう少し伸ばしたいのですが、何か良い方法はありませんか」という学習者の質問に、「日本語の新書でよいから、色々な分野の本を片っ端から読んでごらん」というようなアドバイスをする英語の先生が多いわけです。このようなアドバイスをもらっても「え？日本語ですか。英語のリスニングの話なのですが。先生ちゃんと話を聞いていますか？」などと文句を言ってはいけません。その先生は背景知識のことを考えて、アドバイスをしてくれたのですから。

　ただし、この背景知識を利用した聞き取りにも落とし穴があります。気をつけておかねばならないことは、背景知識に頼り過ぎて話の概略を勝手に作りだしてしまうこと。自分が立てた予想と耳から入ってきた情報に大きな隔たりを感じた時は、背景知識にたよる戦略をすぐさまあきらめて、文法知識の利用など、他の方法を使うようにしましょう。リスニングの際には、方法の柔軟な切り替えも大切です。

Unit 10

Society
■音の変化に慣れよう■

日本を始めとしたいくつかの国では、出生率（birth rate）の低下が大きな社会問題となっています。なぜ出生率は低下するのでしょうか。子育てにお金がかかるからでしょうか。問題はそんなに単純ではないようです。いろいろな理由が複合的に作用しているのかもしれません。一方で、中国やインドでは人口の爆発的増加も懸念されています。「少子化」と「人口爆発」。世界規模でみると、人口問題にも多面性があるようです。

Warm Up 1

CD2-06

よく聞いて、それぞれの写真を一番うまく説明している文を a～d から 1 つ選びなさい。

1.

2.

a b c d

a b c d

First Listening — The Birth Rate

CD2-07

A 会話をよく聞き、質問に答えなさい。

1. Why does Erina enter the apartment?
   - a To talk about the birth rate
   - b To talk to Shan
   - c To wait for Sophie
   - d To have a drink

2. How many brothers and sisters does Shan have?
   - a Two brothers and a sister
   - b A brother and two sisters
   - c A brother and a sister
   - d Two brothers and two sisters

3. What does Erina say about the population?
   - a It might fall to 30% of today's total and 14% of people will be over 65 years old.
   - b It might slowly fall to 90 million and 65% of people will be over 40 years old.
   - c It might fall until 2055 and most people will be over 65 years old.
   - d It might fall to less than 90 million and 40% of people will be over 65 years old.

4. What reasons does Erina suggest for the low birth rate?
   - a Children are expensive and women can't find good jobs.
   - b Children cost a lot of money and women want careers.
   - c Houses are too expensive and women want careers.
   - d Children aren't cheap and women don't want to get married.

Unit 10 Society

B 音の変化に注意しながら会話をよく聞き、下線部をうめなさい（下線１つにつき１語が入ります）。

Shan: Oh, Erina. Hi.
Erina: Hi, Shan. (1) _____ _____ _____ _____ ? Is Sophie in?
Shan: No. She said you were coming round, but (2) _____ _____ _____ _____ _____ _____ a few minutes. She'll be back soon. (3) _____ _____ _____ _____ _____ and wait?
Erina: Okay. Thanks.
Shan: (4) _____ _____ _____ something to drink?
Erina: Thank you. Some tea, please.

Warm Up 2

CD2-08

よく聞いて、a～ｃのうちから一番よい応答に１つ○をしなさい。

1. a   b   c   2. a   b   c

3. a   b   c   4. a   b   c

Second Listening   Why Is It So Low?

CD2-09

A Sophie が言ったことを一番よく描写している文をそれぞれ１つ選びなさい。

1. a   She said that she doesn't understand the meaning of birth rate.
    b   She said that rich countries have the lowest birth rates.
    c   She said that poorer countries can't afford to have high birth rates.

2. a   She said that the population of the world is too high.
    b   She said that she wants only two children.
    c   She said that having fewer children is a big problem.

B Shan が言ったことを一番よく描写している文をそれぞれ 1 つ選びなさい。

1. a He said that he thinks Sophie's ideas are mean.
   b He said that there are many reasons behind the low birth rate.
   c He said that the reasons for the low birth rate don't make sense.

2. a He said women can find it difficult to have children and a career.
   b He said women can't have children and a serious career.
   c He said that bringing up children is more difficult than having a career.

C 音の変化に注意しながら会話をよく聞き、下線部をうめなさい（下線 1 つにつき 1 語が入ります）。

Sophie: What (1) _____ _____ _____ this morning with Erina?

Shan: Oh that! It's (2) _____ _____ _____ think. We were talking about our families and then the low birth rate.

Sophie: Oh right. It's strange, isn't it?

Shan: (3) _____ _____ ?

Sophie: Well, (4) _____ _____ _____ people saying that the low birth rate is because it's so expensive to bring up children.

D 次の質問についてグループでディスカッションをしてみましょう（話を始める前に考えをまとめて、それをメモしなさい）。

1. What do you think are the reasons for the low birth rate?
2. How do you think the birth rate could be increased?

Unit 10 Society

Third Listening — Marriage and Children

CD2-10

A 音の変化に注意しながら会話をよく聞き、下線部をうめなさい（下線１つにつき２語以上が入ります）。

Talking to Erina and Sophie made me think about my own plans ¹._____ future. I've thought a lot about my career, but up until now haven't given much thought to family life.

I'm in no hurry, but I do ²._____ married one day. Perhaps when I'm about 30. I also ³._____ children although I don't mind if they are boys or girls. I think that having just one child is unfair because there is too much pressure ⁴._____ child, so I would prefer two or three. But of course I'd need to discuss it with my partner.

Most Australian women work these days so it is likely that my partner will have a career. Actually, I'd prefer ⁵._____ work. I think it makes a marriage ⁶._____ equal partnership and I definitely want to have an equal role in bringing up my children.

B 将来、どのような家族を持ちたいか、短いパラグラフにまとめなさい。

C Bで書いたパラグラフを使い、自分の考えをクラスに報告しなさい。

Listening Strategy

■音の変化に慣れよう■

　リスニングの際に、英語学習者はとかく音の変化に戸惑うことが多いようです。本来あるべき音が脱落していたり、弱くなっていたり、隣の音とつながって別の音に変わっていたり。どうしてはっきり発音してくれないのかと、イライラすることも多いようです。しかし、これらの音変化は何も英語に限った現象ではありません。以下のように日本語でも同じようなことが起っているのです。

　　　・さんかくけい→さんかっけい
　　　・やっている→やってる

　それではどのように対策を立てれば良いのでしょうか。研究によると、音の変化にはいくつかのパタンがあり、そのパタンを知識として知り、実際に聞いて慣れ、そして発話練習することにより変化に対応できるといいます。

　紙幅の関係ですべてを説明することはできませんが、いくつか代表的な音変化のパターンをここにあげてみましょう。まず、アクセントがこない母音は弱く発音される傾向があります。この傾向は特に語頭で顕著に出ます。たとえば about という単語には母音が２ヶ所ありますが、語頭の /a/ にはアクセントがこないため限りなく弱くなります。したがって、「(ァ) バウト」のように「ア」の音はかすかにしか聞こえなくなります。代名詞の中には、語頭の子音が脱落するものもあり、he は「イ (ー)」、him は「イム」、のように聞こえてきます。また、語尾の子音も弱くなって脱落する例があり、and は「アン」、must は「マス」のように聞こえてきます。さらに、連続する２つの単語の語尾と語頭に同じ音が続く場合は、片方を落す傾向もあります。たとえば top player は、「トッププレイヤー」ではなく「トップレイヤー」のように聞こえることになります。

　連続する単語が混じりあって別の音への変わる例としては、you が前の単語と交じり合い、音が変わるケースがあげられます。たとえば、did you が「ディッド・ユー」ではなく「ディッジュ」、Bless you!（お大事に）が「ブレス・ユー」ではなく「ブレッシュ」となったりします。また to 不定詞が動詞とつながって音変化をおこし、want to が「ワナ」、not going to が「ナッガナ」と聞こえたりします。

　このような音変化のパターンをまとめた参考書もたくさん出版されていますので、ぜひこれらの書籍を使って練習をしてみてください。その際に大切なのは、１）ルールを覚えて、２）何度も聞いて、そして必ず３）発話練習をすることです。

Unit 11

New Year
■固有名詞に着目しよう■

海外に留学するとThanksgiving DayやChristmasなどの大きな祝日にさびしい思いをすることがあります。寮などにいると、ほぼ無人に近い状態となり、なおさらホームシックにかられるもの。そんな時、クラスメイトが自宅のパーティに招いてくれたり、イベントに誘いだしてくれたりすると、とても嬉しいものです。日本ではお盆やお正月になると留学生はさびしい思いをするもの。そんな時、思い切って留学生を誘ってみてはどうでしょうか。

Warm Up 1　　CD2-11

よく聞いて、それぞれの写真を一番うまく説明している文をa～dから1つ選びなさい。

1.

a　b　c　d

2.

a　b　c　d

First Listening — Homesick

🎧 CD2-12

A 会話をよく聞き、質問に答えなさい。

1. Where does Sophie think everyone is?
   - a Shopping
   - b Away on vacation
   - c With their families
   - d In the USA

2. Where does Sophie want to be?
   - a Out with her friends
   - b At home in the UK
   - c Shopping in Kyoto
   - d With Jake's family

3. Where is Shan calling from?
   - a A street corner
   - b A party
   - c The train
   - d His friend's house

4. When will Sophie and Jake meet Shan?
   - a In 15 minutes
   - b In 50 minutes
   - c When they get to the station
   - d When he arrives home

B 会話をもう一度よく聞き、会話中に出てきた固有名詞のリストを完成させなさい（先頭の文字が提示されています）。

Events / Festivals:
1. C_____
2. N_____ _____
3. C_____ _____
4. N____ _____ ____

Places:
5. A_____
6. J_____
7. K_____
8. E_____
9. S_____ _____
10. D_____
11. I_____ and K_____

Company Name:
12. K_____

Warm Up 2   CD2-13

よく聞いて、a〜cのうちから一番よい応答に1つ○をしなさい。

1. a b c   2. a b c

3. a b c   4. a b c

Second Listening   Hatsumode

🎧 CD2-14

A Sophie が言ったことを一番よく描写している文をそれぞれ1つ選びなさい。

1.
   a   She said that Shan told her about the ESS.
   b   She said that she sometimes goes to help the ESS too.
   c   She said that she had a really good time at Christmas.

2.
   a   She said that Daiki gave his girlfriend a romantic Christmas present.
   b   She said that the present Daiki gave his girlfriend was too practical.
   c   She said that Daiki should have spent more money at Christmas.

B Daiki が言ったことを一番よく描写している文をそれぞれ1つ選びなさい。

1.
   a   He said that his girlfriend paid for the fried chicken.
   b   He said that eating fried chicken is romantic.
   c   He said that he only eats fried chicken at Christmas.

2.
   a   He said that he will try to be romantic next Christmas.
   b   He said that Sophie should feel sorry for him.
   c   He said that he can't afford to be romantic.

C 会話をもう一度よく聞き、会話中に出てきた固有名詞のリスト（左側）を完成させなさい。その後、完成したリストの固有名詞を、それぞれ正しい説明（右側）と線で結びつけなさい。

1.   E_____-S_____ S_____   ・   ・ the first shrine visit of the year
2.   H_____   ・   ・ a university circle
3.   C_____   ・   ・ a food eaten at Christmas
4.   C_____ P_____   ・   ・ a believer in Jesus Christ

D 次の質問についてグループでディスカッションをしてみましょう（話を始める前に考えをまとめて、それをメモしなさい）。

1.   What things do you think are romantic?
2.   What will you wish for at New Year?

Unit 11 New Year

Third Listening — Christmas Memories

CD2-15

A ある単語の末尾と次の単語の先頭に同じ子音がきた場合、音が聞き取り難くなります。この点に留意して下線部をうめなさい。

I really enjoyed spending Christmas and New Year in Japan even though it was not at 1._____ the festive season at home.

In England, Christmas is a time for families to 2._____ . My grandmother used to come and stay with us on Christmas Eve and then my aunties, uncles and cousins would come to visit on Christmas Day.

Everyone exchanged presents. I got gifts 3._____ brothers and sisters, from my parents and grandparents, and even from my aunties and uncles. I've got a big family so I used to get so many gifts.

We spent Christmas Day playing with our new toys. Mum would spend all morning in the kitchen cooking the turkey for Christmas dinner. Then all the family would get together to eat at 4._____ o'clock. I used to love Christmas. It was the 5._____ of the year for me.

B 子どもの頃、家族とどのように新年を過ごしたか、短いパラグラフにまとめなさい。

C Bで書いたパラグラフを使い、自分の経験をクラスに報告しなさい。

Listening Strategy

■固有名詞に着目しよう■

　固有名詞（地名や人名、企業名など）というのは、リスニングにおいて意外と理解の阻害要因となりがちなものです。その理由は、日本語で慣れ親しんでいる発音と英語の発音が大きく異なるからです。たとえば、私たちは、中国の首都を「ペキン」と覚えていますが、英語の発音では Beijing「ベイジン」と聞こえてきます。「サイプラス」という地名は一体どこのことかと考えていると実は Cyprus「キプロス」（地中海に浮かぶ島国）であったりするのです。さらには、「キオト」とはどこの外国の地名かと思えば、日本の「京都」のことだった、という笑い話もあります。以下にこのような紛らわしい都市名や国名を数例あげておきますので、どこの国名あるいは都市名なのか考えてみてください。

　　Athens, Berlin, Geneva, Georgia, Greece, Prague, Vienna, Warsaw

　同様にして人名や企業名も結構やっかいなものです。たとえば、「イミョンバク」といわれて韓国大統領の「李明博」をすぐに思いだすには、英語での国際ニュースに対して相当な慣れが必要でしょう。同じように、「マオツートン」などといわれると見当もつかないかもしれませんが、中華人民共和国の建国の父である「毛沢東」のことになります。ちなみに、「フーチンタオ」というと、現在、中国の最高指導者である「胡錦涛」です。
　企業名では、「ナイコン」という会社名は日本のカメラメーカーの１つである「ニコン」であったり、「ハンダ」は日本の自動車メーカの「ホンダ」であったり、「ヒュンダイ」は韓国の「現代」グループであったりします。
　厄介なことに、ニュースなどで取り扱われる固有名詞は、毎日、次々と増えていきます。しかし、固有名詞がわかると、トピックの推測がある程度できるようになり、話のあらすじを追っていくことが容易になるので、出来るだけ毎日、新聞を読み、この発音は英語だったらどういうのだろう、と意識して覚えるようにしてください。

（答）アセンス（アテネ：ギリシャの首都）、バーリン（ベルリン：ドイツの首都）、ジニーバ（ジュネーブ：スイスの都市名）、ジョージア（グルジア共和国あるいは米国のジョージア州）、グリース（ギリシャ：国名）、プラーグ（プラハ：チェコの首都）、ヴィエナ（ウイーン：オーストリアの首都）、ワルソー（ワルシャワ：ポーランドの首都）

Unit 12

Clean Living
■視覚情報を利用しよう■

みんなが裸で入る銭湯（public bath）と聞くと、顔をしかめる留学生もいるようです。でも、When in Rome, do as the Romans do.（郷に入れば郷に従え）という諺があるように、なんでも挑戦してみることが大切です。そうすれば、思いがけない面白いことが体験できるはず。異文化体験では（非合法なこと以外は）尻込みしないで挑戦することが何よりも大切。みなさんも留学生を誘って、日本文化（留学生にとっての異文化）の案内役になってみてはどうでしょうか？

Warm Up 1
CD2-16

よく聞いて、それぞれの写真を一番うまく説明している文をa～dから1つ選びなさい。

1.

a   b   c   d

2.

a   b   c   d

First Listening: Visiting a Bathhouse

CD2-17

A 会話をよく聞き、質問に答えなさい。

1. Why is Sophie going to a bathhouse?
    a   She is dirty and needs a bath.
    b   There isn't a bathroom in her apartment.
    c   Her water heater at home isn't working.
    d   She has something to talk about with Erina.

2. What plans has Sophie made for going home?
    a   She has made a lot.
    b   She has made some.
    c   She has made only one.
    d   She hasn't made any.

3. How does Sophie feel about leaving Japan?
    a   She's looking forward to it.
    b   She feels she could stay longer.
    c   She's excited about going home.
    d   She feels like coming back to Japan.

4. What doesn't Sophie want to think about?
    a   Searching for a job.
    b   Flying to England.
    c   Looking for a new apartment.
    d   Finishing her school work in Japan.

Unit 12　Clean Living

B イラストを利用しながら、もう一度よく会話を聞き、ボックスの中の単語を使って下線部をうめなさい。

| tap | bowl | basket | stool |

1. Put your clothes in a _____ .
2. Bring a _____ to sit on and a plastic _____ over to the shower.
3. … you can turn the cold _____ on for a moment.

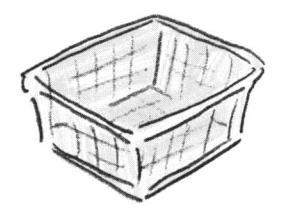

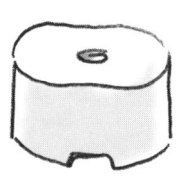

Warm Up 2　　　CD2-18

よく聞いて、a～c のうちから一番よい応答に1つ○をしなさい。

1.　a　b　c　　　　2.　a　b　c

3.　a　b　c　　　　4.　a　b　c

Second Listening　Showers and Baths

CD2-19

A Jake が言ったことを一番よく描写している文をそれぞれ1つ選びなさい。

1. a　He said that he'll go to the bathhouse tomorrow.
   b　He said that he doesn't need to take showers when it's cold.
   c　He said that he'll take a shower when the water heater is repaired.

2. a　He said that he would not enjoy visiting the bathhouse.
   b　He said that he's not nervous about visiting the bathhouse.
   c　He said that it's really strange to go to a bathhouse.

B Sophie が言ったことを一番よく描写している文をそれぞれ１つ選びなさい。

1. a   She said that the bathhouse is nearby and cheap.
   b   She said that the bathhouse is far away but not expensive.
   c   She said that the bathhouse is far away and costs too much.

2. a   She said that she likes a shower in the evening.
   b   She said that she needs a shower to relax.
   c   She said that she needs a shower every day.

C 下の語句を使って、写真の吹き出しの Sophie と Jake の会話を完成させなさい。

a	Oh, thanks!	(1.)
b	I can lend you my bowl.	(2.)
c	OK, but you'd smell a lot nicer if you did go.	(3.)
d	To the *sento*. It's a public bathhouse.	(4.)
e	To the what?	(5.)
f	I don't want to borrow it.	(6.)

D 次の質問についてグループでディスカッションをしてみましょう（話を始める前に考えをまとめて、それをメモしなさい）。

1. Jake always takes a shower and thinks that baths are boring. What do you think?

2. Sophie really enjoyed going to the bathhouse. What do you think of public baths?

Unit 12 Clean Living

Third Listening — How Embarrassing!

🎧 CD2-20

A /s/ と /ʃ/ の音の違いに注意しながら、"s" で始まる単語で下線部をうめなさい。

I have had to change some of my habits ¹._____ I came to Japan and it hasn't always been easy.

Everybody knows that the Japanese don't wear ²._____ inside. It has been fairly easy to follow that rule, but with toilet ³._____ it's another ⁴._____. I remember going to a friend's for dinner. I went to the bathroom and then came back to the table. I couldn't work out why everyone was looking at me. Finally, I looked down at my feet and realized I was ⁵._____ wearing the toilet slippers. I was ⁶._____ embarrassed.

Another time I was on the train. I was hungry so I pulled a ⁷._____ out of my bag and ⁸._____ to eat. The friend I was with looked uncomfortable but I didn't know why. ⁹._____ told me later that it is bad manners to eat on the train — though for ¹⁰._____ reason the *Shinkansen* is different and you can eat as much as you want.

B 人前で恥ずかしい思いをした経験について、短いパラグラフにまとめなさい。

C Bで書いたパラグラフを使い、自分の経験をクラスに報告しなさい。

Listening Strategy

■視覚情報を利用しよう■

　リスニングは耳からの情報だけに頼るものと考えがちですが、実は目からの情報もかなりの手助けになります。たとえば、発話者の頭の動き。英語を話す時は、アクセントのある単語や重要な語句と同期して、人の頭は動くものです。ためしに、CNN や BBC などのキャスターの頭の動き、あるいは米国大統領の演説中の頭の動きなどを観察してみましょう。重要な概念がどこなのか、ある程度は推測することができるはずです。

　また、手の動きもたくさんの情報を我々に伝えてくれます。たとえば、難しい概念を述べる時には、人は何かをつかむようなジェスチャー（これをバトン・ジェスチャーといいます）や、何かを下から受けるようなジェスチャーをすることが多いと言われています。さらに、人の話を引用する時には、クオテーション・マーク（引用符）を宙に書くようなジェスチャーをします。こんなところに着目するだけで、リスニングはかなり楽になるものです。

　ただ、視覚情報の利用には注意も必要です。たとえば、ビデオの映像は確かにはたくさんの情報を伝えてくれますが、そればかりに注意を奪われてしまい、肝心の耳からの情報をおろそかにしてしまう傾向が強いと指摘されています。なんとなくわかったつもりになっても、実はそれは映像のおかげであり、映像を取り去ると重要なところは相変わらず聞き取れていない、ということもよくおこります。したがって、音声情報にのみ集中する機会を設けるなど、うまく工夫して映像を利用していく必要があるようです。また字幕（日本語、英語）も、使い方を誤るとリスニング力を伸ばす手助けにはならないようです。なぜなら、人間は文字が出てくると、そちらへ注意が引きつけられ、それを読むことに多くの注意資源を費やす傾向があるからです。こうなると、肝心の耳からの情報の処理に注意力が割けない分、リスニングには不利になります。英語字幕を利用してリスニングの練習をしていたら、リスニング力には変化はなかったがリーディング力が伸びた、という噴飯ものの研究結果も報告されているので、字幕の安易な利用は考えものです。

Unit 13

A Change in the Weather
■語彙を増やそう■

地球の温暖化（global warming）が大きな問題になっている昨今。みなさんも、少しでも違いを生み出すために、レジ袋（plastic bag）を節約したり、車の利用を控えたり、いろんな努力を重ねておられることでしょう。そのような努力のひとつに、エアコンの利用自粛や温度制限というのがあります。ただこれは、日本の夏の暑さを考えた時、かなりの我慢を強いることになるので、留学生たちの間でも賛否両論があるようです。

Warm Up 1
CD2-21

よく聞いて、それぞれの写真を一番うまく説明している文をa〜dから1つ選びなさい。

1.

2.

a b c d

a b c d

First Listening — At the ESS

A 会話をよく聞き、質問に答えなさい。

1. What do we learn about Adelaide?
   - a It's in the north of Australia.
   - b It's the biggest city in Australia.
   - c It's a planned city.
   - d It doesn't have a lot of space.

2. What kind of place is Barossa?
   - a A park
   - b A city
   - c A hill
   - d A valley

3. What can we infer about winter in Australia?
   - a It's in January.
   - b It's in February.
   - c It's in July.
   - d It's in November.

4. What does Shan NOT mention about the sun?
   - a Keep out of the sun.
   - b Wear a shirt when you swim.
   - c Wear a hat when you go outside.
   - d Put on sun cream.

Unit 13 A Change in the Weather

B もう一度会話をよく聞き、下線部をアルファベットの文字でうめて単語を完成させなさい。その後、a～cから話の正しい定義を1つ選び意味を確認しなさい。

1. There are five _ _ j _ r cities in Australia,

   a capital   b lively   c large

2. ... it's all _ t _ _ _ g _ t roads and there's lots of parkland.

   a wide   b unbending   c scenic

3. ... the seasons are the _ _ _ o _ i _ e of what you're used to, ...

   a reverse   b symbol   c epitome

Warm Up 2   CD2-23

よく聞いて、a～cのうちから一番よい応答に1つ○をしなさい。

1. a   b   c   2. a   b   c

3. a   b   c   4. a   b   c

Second Listening   The Climate

CD2-24

A Shan が言ったことを一番よく描写している文をそれぞれ1つ選びなさい。

1. a   He said that he will be back in Australia in the summer.
    b   He said that it will be autumn when he gets back to Australia.
    c   He said that he wants to go back to Australia in the winter.

2. a   He said that he used to get through the summer without using air-conditioners.
    b   He said that Australians have never needed air-conditioners in summer.
    c   He said that he feels comfortable when he turns the air conditioner off.

B Jakeが言ったことを一番よく描写している文をそれぞれ1つ選びなさい。

1. a He said that the summer in Japan was humid.
   b He said that the summer in Japan was hot.
   c He said that the summer in Japan was too long.

2. a He said that air-conditioners in America are different.
   b He said that they have always had air-conditioners in America.
   c He said that an air-conditioner is better than a *kotatsu*.

C もう一度会話をよく聞き、下線部をうめて単語を完成させなさい。その後、a〜cから語の正しい定義を1つ選び意味を確認しなさい。

1. We were fighting about which heat _ e _ ti _ _ we should use.
   a temperature
   b device
   c switch

2. Yeah, you're all very _ _ m _ o _ _ ab _ e ...
   a busy
   b rich
   c relaxed

3. But nobody knew about the problem of _ l _ _ a _ warming ...
   a incredible
   b worldwide
   c unbelievable

D 次の質問についてグループでディスカッションをしてみましょう（話を始める前に考えをまとめて、それをメモしなさい）。

1. Which season do you like best? Why do you like it?
2. How do you use your air-conditioner?

Unit 13 A Change in the Weather

Third Listening — Climate Change

CD2-25

A "ch" と "sh" の表す音に注意しながら、下線部をうめなさい。

Meeting the ESS students made me think again about ^{1.}_____ in the world's weather. Of course, I studied about climate change at school and know that global warming is a real ^{2.}_____ . I also think I ^{3.}_____ personally try and do something about it.

Back in Australia, there has been one of the longest droughts ever. In some parts of the country it has not rained for years so the animals have died, and some farmers have had no ^{4.}_____ but to leave their land. There are often water ^{5.}_____ , even in the cities, and the situation is getting worse.

Australians these days rarely go outside without a hat or sun ^{6.}_____ and sun cream, so it was a ^{7.}_____ for me to see some people in Japan out in the sun in the middle of the day. Also, many students here went sunbathing last summer, which my parents never let me do.

B 以下のどちらかのトピックで短いパラグラフを１つ書きなさい。

1. 地球温暖化（Global warming）を防ぐために個人でできること
2. 太陽の紫外線（Ultraviolet rays）から身を守る方法

C Bで書いたパラグラフを使い、自分の考えをクラスに報告しなさい。

Listening Strategy

■語彙を増やそう■

　みなさんの英語の語彙量はどの程度あるでしょうか？2,000語、3,000語？あるいは5,000語でしょうか？研究によると2,000語程度の語彙があると、日常会話の約95％をカバーできると言います。ただ、我々が遭遇するのは日常会話ばかりではありません。英語による講義やニュースを聞くためには、2,000語ではまったく足りません。ましてや学術書を読む場合などになると、2,000語ではまったくお手上げです。たしかに、Unit 4 や Unit 9 のコラムで説明したように、全部聞き取らずに背景知識を利用して未知語を推測することは可能です。それでも、20語につき1語程度知らない単語が出てくる場合の話しで、これを越えてしまうと、もう推測することも不可能になります。だからこそ、我々は語彙を増やしていかねばならないのです。では、どのようにすれば語彙は増やせるのでしょうか。ここでは2つほど方法をご紹介しましょう。

　第1番目の方法としては、多重経路を利用する方法です。人は目からのみ情報を入れたり、耳からのみ情報を入れたりすると、その情報はなかなか定着しないものです。しかし、複数の経路から情報を入れると、定着率は格段に上がります。声に出す、スペルを書く、動作をつけるなどのモードを複合的に利用すると、特に有効なようです。また、例文に埋め込んで覚えると活用範囲も広がります。

　第2番目の方法は、語幹や接辞を利用する方法です。たとえば、ex- という接辞が「前の」「切り離された」などを意味するということを知れば、ex-wife は「前妻」であり、excommunication は「コミュニケーションを切り離す」から転じて「破門」というような意味になることが推測できます。同じように -cide は「殺す」という意味であることを押さえておくと、pesticide, insecticide, homicide, suicide などの語の意味を簡単に覚えることができます。

　これ以外にもいろいろな方法がありますので、良い方法を自分なりに考え、試行錯誤をしながら、語彙を増やす努力を続けてみてください。

Unit 14

Packing Up
■数の表現に注意しよう■

留学生たちは帰国が近づくと、航空券の手配、家具の処分、荷造りと忙しくなります。原油高の昨今、航空運賃には、税金の他にサーチャージ（oil surcharge）もついて高くなりがち。それでもなんとか航空券を手配できたら、次は家具類の処分です。Unit 3 とは逆の手順で、インターネットなどを使い少しでも高く売って、航空運賃の足しにしたいところです。最後は荷造りですが、この頃になると時間が足りずパニックになりがち。ぜひ、お手伝いしてあげたいものです。

Warm Up 1
CD2-26

よく聞いて、それぞれの写真を一番うまく説明している文を a～d から1つ選びなさい。

1.

2.

a　b　c　d　　　　a　b　c　d

First Listening   Farewell Party

CD2-27

A 会話をよく聞き、質問に答えなさい。

1. Where are Sophie and Daiki?
   a In a restaurant in Kyoto
   b In Sophie, Jake and Shan's apartment
   c In Daiki's apartment
   d In Helsinki, the capital city of Finland

2. Why didn't Sophie buy the cheapest ticket home?
   a Because she wants to go to Helsinki.
   b Because she doesn't want to visit Bangkok.
   c Because the airline wasn't safe.
   d Because the flying time was longer.

3. How is Jake going to get all his stuff back to the States?
   a Fly with some and post the rest.
   b Post it all.
   c Pay the extra cost and take it all.
   d Fly with some of it and leave the rest.

4. Why is the sofa still in the apartment?
   a Because the buyer hasn't paid yet.
   b Because it hasn't been picked up yet.
   c Because the buyer will move in tomorrow.
   d Because it hasn't been sold yet.

Unit 14 Packing Up

B 数に注意して会話を聞き、下線部を埋めなさい。

1. From Sophie and Daiki's conversation:
   Sophie's ticket cost _____ yen. She could have saved _____ yen going home via Bangkok.

2. From Jake and Erina's conversation:
   If Jake took all his luggage with him it would be _____ kilograms over the limit. He would have to pay an extra _____ yen.

3. From Shan and Emi's conversation:
   They paid _____ yen for the sofa a year ago.
   Shan sold it on the internet for _____ yen.

Warm Up 2
CD2-28

よく聞いて、a～c のうちから一番よい応答に1つ○をしなさい。

1. a b c   2. a b c

3. a b c   4. a b c

Second Listening So Much Stuff!

CD2-29

A Sophie が言ったことを一番よく描写している文をそれぞれ1つ選びなさい。

1. a She said that she is going to help Shan sell the stuff online.
   b She said that she can't stop panicking about the rubbish.
   c She said that most of the stuff left in the apartment is trash.

2. a She said that she has never dropped rubbish on the street.
   b She said that Jake is talking a lot of rubbish.
   c She said that they should make a deal with their landlord.

B Jake が言ったことを一番よく描写している文をそれぞれ1つ選びなさい。

1. a   He said that Shan made a profit when he sold the microwave.
    b   He said that Shan has sold the sofa, microwave and table.
    c   He said that Shan has sold the table back to the recycling shop.

2. a   He said that the landlord will throw all their stuff away for them.
    b   He said that he will ask the landlord to throw their stuff away.
    c   He said that their stuff is the landlord's responsibility.

C 数に注意して会話を聞き、下線部を適語（数）でうめなさい。

1. When are they leaving?
    In _____ hours.

2. How much did Shan sell the microwave for?
    For _____ yen.

3. How much profit did Shan make on the table?
    He made _____ yen.

4. How much does Sophie say they will save by leaving their rubbish behind?
    Maybe _____ yen.

5. How much will they pay the recycle shop to take their stuff away?
    They will pay _____ yen.

D 次の質問についてグループでディスカッションをしてみましょう（話を始める前に考えをまとめて、それをメモしなさい）。

1. What would you do in Sophie and Jake's situation?
2. Have you ever dropped trash on the street? What kind of trash?

Third Listening — Presents

A /v/ と /f/ の音に注意して下線部をうめなさい。

CD2-30

I had so many things to take back from Japan. At least 1._____ of them were presents for my friends and family.

For my mom, I bought a wallet. It's made of what the Japanese call *koshu inden* and has a 2._____ pattern. She uses it every day. I also bought her a tea set of 3._____ cups and a teapot. She 4._____ it.

I bought my dad some pictures. He's liked art all his 5._____ so I got him some Japanese woodblock prints. My 6._____ one is of a samurai drinking *sake*. It's now hanging in the 7._____ room at my parents' house.

The biggest present was a *shamisen*, a musical instrument, for my sister. It's what she really wanted. You can 8._____ them in the States but she wanted a genuine Japanese one. Anyway, she is delighted with it so that's fine.

B 今までにあなたが友人や家族に贈ったプレゼントに関して、何を贈ったのか、どうしてそれを選んだのかを含んで、短いパラグラフにまとめなさい。

C B で書いたパラグラフを使い、自分の体験をクラスに報告しなさい。

Listening Strategy

■数の表現に注意しよう■

　TOEIC® をはじめとした英語テストでは、数字を聞き取らせたり、聞き取った数字を組み合わせて簡単な計算をさせたりという問題が出題されることがあります。このような問題が多く出題されるのは、英語学習者が不得手とする分野の1つに数の聞き取りがあるので、そこを試してみようとする意図が出題者の側に生じるからなのでしょう。これを裏返して言えば、数字が出てきた場合には、その部分が聞き取りのポイントになっている場合が多いということにもなります。

　そこで、以下に数の英語に関する表現のルールをいくつか紹介して、みなさんに苦手意識克服に取り組んでいただきましょう。ただし、ルールをいくら覚えても、聞き取りが容易になるわけではありません。実際は、何度も繰り返して聞き取り練習と発話練習をして、無意識にそのルールに従って反応できるように準備しておく必要があることをお忘れなく。

　まずは桁数の多い数字の場合です。英語の場合、3つずつかためて読み、あとは単位をつけていくだけで読み上げることができます。つまり、下の例は 145 billion, 678 million, 299 thousand, 215 と読めば良いということになります。145 は one hundred forty five ですので、この要領ですべてを読み上げると、one hundred forty five billion, six hundred seventy eight million, two hundred ninety nine thousand, two hundred (and) fifteen dollars となっていきます。

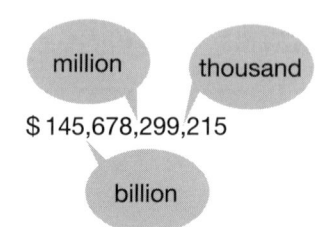

$ 145,678,299,215
　　billion　million　thousand

　小数点以下がある場合は、「.」をポイントとよみ、以下は1つずつ読み上げます。たとえば、3.14 は three point one four, 0.17 は zero point one seven となるわけです。分数は、分子から分母へと読み、分子は普通の数字（基数）の読み方、分母は順番をあらわす序数の読み方となります。従って、3/7 は three-sevenths となります。ただし、1/2 や 1/4 はそれぞれ、a half や a quarter と読む場合もあるので注意が必要です（たとえば 3/4 は three-quarters）。時間の場合は、基本的には、twenty minutes past eleven（11時20分）のように読みますが、たとえば、10時15分は a quarter past ten、9時45分は a quarter to ten となったりするところに注意が必要です。

Unit 15

Back Home
■多様な題材をいろいろな人の声で聞いてみよう■

留学先から母国へ帰っても、外国語の学習は続けていけるものです。特に、インターネットがここまで発達すれば、ネイティブスピーカーがいないとか、教材がないとか、書く機会や読む機会がないとかいうのは、すこしも言い訳になりません。コンピュータなどのメディアを賢く使って、自発的に学習を進めていきましょう。先人が言うように「継続は力なり」(Continuity is the father of success.) なのですから。

Warm Up 1　　CD2-31

よく聞いて、それぞれの写真を一番うまく説明している文を a～d から1つ選びなさい。

1.

2.

a　b　c　d　　　　a　b　c　d

First Listening — A Video Chat

CD2-32

A 会話をよく聞き、質問に答えなさい。

1. Where are Sophie, Jake and Shan?
   a Back in Japan a year later
   b On vacation in Australia
   c Back in their home countries
   d At a reunion party in America

2. How does Shan feel about being home?
   a Australia feels real.   b He feels different.
   c It feels like a dream.   d Being home feels weird.

3. Will Jake continue studying Japanese?
   a No, his college has no Japanese class.
   b Yes, he will study on his own.
   c No, he's too busy on the internet.
   d Yes, if he can find a teacher.

4. Why does Jake want to keep in touch with Sophie?
   a Because he likes her more than anyone.
   b Because the world is so interconnected.
   c Because he thinks she is a great person.
   d Because he enjoys fighting with her.

Unit 15　Back Home

B もう一度聞いて、会話中で触れられている項目をチェック（✓）しなさい。

1. _____ making cheap international phone calls
2. _____ watching TV programs
3. _____ using a social networking site
4. _____ reading and writing blogs
5. _____ downloading audio and video files
6. _____ reading online editions of newspapers
7. _____ video chatting
8. _____ studying university courses online.

Warm Up 2

CD2-35

よく聞いて、a～c のうちから一番よい応答に１つ○をしなさい。

1.　a　b　c　　　　　2.　a　b　c

3.　a　b　c　　　　　4.　a　b　c

Second Listening　Language Learning

CD2-36

A Sophie が言ったことを一番よく描写している文をそれぞれ１つ選びなさい。

1. a　She said that French is different from Japanese.
   b　She said that French is often similar to Japanese.
   c　She said that she wishes that she had studied French.

2. a　She said that a lot of her friends in Japan were from England.
   b　She said that a lot of her Japanese friends were English speakers.
   c　She said that in Japan she only made friends with English speakers.

B David が言ったことを一番よく描写している文をそれぞれ 1 つ選びなさい。

1. a   He said that he worked in France for six months.
   b   He said that he lived in France for half a year.
   c   He said that he spent all his money in France.

2. a   He said that he used a variety of materials to learn French.
   b   He said that he insisted on speaking French in France.
   c   He said that he was interested in speaking the local language in France.

C Sophie が会話中で触れた項目をチェック（✓）しなさい。

1. _____ She listened to lectures.
2. _____ She read the newspapers.
3. _____ She went to karaoke.
4. _____ She watched local Japanese TV.
5. _____ She listened to Japanese music.
6. _____ She played music.
7. _____ She listened to audiobooks.
8. _____ She watched Japanese films.
9. _____ She read *manga*.

D 次の質問についてグループでディスカッションをしてみましょう（話を始める前に考えをまとめて、それをメモしなさい）。

1. What materials have you used to study English?
2. Which languages do you think are easiest for Japanese people to learn? Why?

Unit 15 Back Home

Third Listening — What Else Did I Learn?

🎧 CD2-37

A /l/ と /r/ の違いに注意して選択肢からどちらか適当な語を選びなさい。

After talking to David the other day about studying Japanese I wondered what else I'd learnt from my year in Japan. I sat down and wrote a ^{1.}**(wrist/list)** of every idea I could think of.

At the top is friendship. I lived with Shan and Jake for a year, almost like a family. Of course, our personalities often ^{2.}**(clashed/crashed)** but despite that we came to rely on each other. I can't imagine what my ^{3.}**(life/rife)** in Japan would have been like without them.

From my relationships with Japanese people I learnt that there is more than one way to see the world. I think I returned from Japan a more mature, open-minded and tolerant individual. I definitely ^{4.}**(grew/glue)** as a person over there.

^{5.}**(Finery/Finally)** I learnt a lot about England, too. People say that you only truly understand your own country when you have seen it from a distance. I think they are ^{6.}**(light/right)**.

B 自分が個人的な体験から外国語学習に関して学んだことを何か１つ短いパラグラフにまとめなさい。

C Bで書いたパラグラフを使い、自分の経験をクラスに報告しなさい。

Listening Strategy

■多様な題材をいろいろな人の声で聞いてみよう■

　おもしろい実験があります。特定の人物1名に吹き込ませた教材を英語学習者にあたえて、一定期間繰り返しリスニングの練習をさせます。その後、同じ人物に吹き込ませたリスニング・テストをやらせると、そこそこの成績がでます。しかし、別の人物に吹き込ませた同じようなレベルのリスニング・テストを受けさせると、前のテストと比べて、なんと成績が下がってしまうことがある、というのです。

　どうしてこんなことがおこるのでしょうか。人の声にはそれぞれ個性（たとえば、高さ、長さ、抑揚、速さ）があり、この個性になれてくると、聞きやすくなる傾向があります。学習者たちも、一定期間の繰り返し学習で吹き込み者の声の個性に慣れていき、馴染みの声となって聞きやすくなったのでしょう。しかし、個性というぐらいですので、人それぞれ違います。当然、別の人には別の個性があるわけで、別のテストでは慣れがかえって邪魔をして、なんだか聞きづらいという感じが出てしまったのでしょう。上述の実験では、恐らくは、このような物理的（そして心理的）な要因が影響して、テストの成績を下げたのだと考えられます。

　ここから言えることは、同じ人物の発話ばかり聞いていては、せっかくの練習の効果が別の場面へ転移しない危険性があるということ。できるだけいろんな個性（出身地、性別、年齢、性格）をもった人の声を聞いて、汎用性のある英語リスニング力を身につけていきたいものです。これと関連して、リスニングの場面（ジャンル）なども聞き取り力に影響することがわかっています。たとえば、大学の講義や大統領の演説のような比較的フォーマルな場面での聞き取り練習ばかりしていると、パーティでの会話や友人同士の電話での会話のようなインフォーマルな場面での聞き取りが苦手になってくるのです。このような場合の対策は、声の個性への対策と同様、意識的にいろいろな場面での発話を聞くしかありません。オールラウンドな英語力をつけたいのであれば、いろいろな場面で英語を聞くこと。そして、もし特定のテスト(TOEFL®など)でのリスニング力をつけたいのであれば、それにあわせた題材を集中的に聞くこと。リスニング力養成には、目的にあわせて戦略（ストラテジー）を選択することが大切なのです。

Listening Partner
An Intermediate Course
―異文化交流のリスニング―

2009 年 1 月 10 日　初版第 1 刷発行
2024 年 2 月 20 日　初版第 11 刷発行

著　者　　竹　内　　理
　　　　　Graeme Todd
　　　　　Roger Palmer

発行者　　福　岡　正　人
発行所　　株式会社　金星堂
（〒101-0051）東京都千代田区神田神保町 3-21
　　　　Tel. (03) 3263-3828（営業部）
　　　　　　(03) 3263-3997（編集部）
　　　　Fax (03) 3263-0716
　　　　https://www.kinsei-do.co.jp

編集担当　芦川正宏　　　　　　　Printed in Japan
印刷所・製本所／日経印刷株式会社
落丁・乱丁本はお取り替えいたします。
本書の内容を無断で複写・複製することを禁じます。
ISBN978-4-7647-3878-2　C1082